Word Weaving

Word Weaving

A Creative Approach to Teaching and Writing Poetry

David M. Johnson
University of New Mexico

National Council of Teachers of English
1111 Kenyon Road, Urbana, Illinois 61801

Cover Design: Doug Burnett

Interior Design: Tom Kovacs for TGK Design

Staff Editor: Tim Bryant

NCTE Stock Number 58226-3020

Library of Congress Cataloging-in-Publication Data
Johnson, David M., 1939–
    Word weaving : a creative approach to teaching and writing poetry
  / David M. Johnson.
        p.   cm.
    Includes bibliographical references.
    ISBN 0-8141-5822-6
    1. Poetry—Study and teaching. 2. Poetry—Authorship. I. Title.
PN1101.J64   1990
808.1—dc20   90-39980
                                                                  CIP

Contents

v

Preface

Every person is special and feels the need to express this uniqueness. Everyone has a song and a story.

Human beings also need community, a web of relationships, a pattern of meaning and purpose. Communities are woven together through songs and stories.

This book is about the imagination and about the role that poetry plays in peoples' lives. This book is about the creativity that produces songs and stories and is the vehicle for self-expression and relationship.

Creativity shows up in every human pursuit, from cabinetmaking to goldsmithing, from quilting to gardening—wherever the imagination is used to create connections between one person and another, between human beings and nature or the cosmos. Creativity is important throughout our lives, in the particular ways we express ourselves and in the bonds we build and maintain with the world.

Some people have problems with the word *creativity*, as if it represented an alien or exotic activity in the practical world of business and technology. Many adults deny their own creativity, choosing to associate this process with a tiny minority of the population, usually dead, who were or are artists living on the fringes of everyday, normal society. These feelings are accentuated with the prospect of writing or reading poetry. Important educational and social issues are raised by these attitudes.

Invariably, the children I meet in elementary school are creative: they write poems, novels, and plays, paint pictures, produce musicals, and sculpt. A nearby elementary school has an annual art night, where artworks of every conceivable kind and medium fill the school, hanging from ceilings and walls, covering tables and doorways. The air is charged with energy, and parents walk around with big smiles on their faces. The children create a multitude of worlds, kaleidoscopic reflections of their dreams and delights, their fears and nightmares—the significant roles for art of any kind, at any age.

So the inevitable question: what happens to this ability, to this energy? Somewhere during maturation, in the educational process and training, children unlearn creativity. Or is it lost through neglect? Eventually, students become "practical" and adult. Most become spectators and consumers, while literature and art and music are left to experts and specialists. Nevertheless, we are living in an enormously inventive and creative age, if we may characterize the energy and ability behind the exploration of space, the development of new products, and the marketing of fad and fashion.

Of the many materials available for creative use, language is common to all people, and at the foundation of the imaginative use of language is poetry. From earliest times poems have captured the cries of the human heart, as well as our visions of a perfect society. Walt Whitman, the father of American poetry, envisioned a boisterous, pluralistic democracy, where saws and hammers, tugboats and trains, males and females of all colors and classes, would hum and buzz with the basic sounds and rhythms of poetry.

Today, however, poetry has an even heavier burden to carry than the more general notions of creativity. Poetry doesn't sell, teachers often avoid it if it's *modern*, students confuse it with cod liver oil and tetanus shots, and parents wonder why poets don't get real jobs.

Despite poetry's negative reputation, there are more poets writing and publishing than ever before. The air is filled with lyrics from radio and TV, records and tapes. Poetry is put to use on bumper stickers, in media commercials, in graffiti on city walls, and in slogans for political candidates and fund-raising campaigns.

Most young people—and old—may not be *reading* poetry in books, but they are hearing it and seeing it, driving and jogging to it, buying and dancing to it. This abundance of poetry provides teachers with an excellent meeting ground with students and, in turn, provides an avenue to other writers, living and dead.

The purpose of this book is to make poetry more accessible: all those poems within each of us yearning for expression, all those poems by others waiting for us to experience them. It is our responsibility to take the materials at hand—the inner world of mythic voices and dark mysteries, and the outer world of beaming sunflowers and stainless steel—and create a home for ourselves: a place where we are reconciled with each other and with earth and sky. In "A Noiseless Patient Spider," Whitman uses weaving as a model for this process:

A noiseless patient spider,
I mark'd where on a little promontory it stood isolated,
Mark'd how to explore the vacant vast surrounding,
It launch'd forth filament, filament, filament, out of itself,
Ever unreeling them, ever tirelessly speeding them.
And you O soul where you stand,
Surrounded, detached, in measureless oceans of space,
Ceaselessly musing, venturing, throwing, seeking the spheres to
     connect them,
Till the bridge you will need be form'd, till the ductile anchor
     hold,
Till the gossamer thread you fling catch somewhere, O my soul.

Acknowledgments

This book has its roots in my own teaching and in my visits to numerous middle school and high school English classes in the Poetry in the Schools program, sponsored by the National Endowment for the Arts and directed in New Mexico by Stanley Noyes. I want to thank Ken Betzen, Carolyn Tuttle, Pat Smith, and Christian Westphal—fine teachers all—for critiquing the manuscript and focusing on its usefulness for teachers. Barrett Price's thoughtful suggestions helped me focus the early chapters. I am grateful to Marta Field for typing the original manuscript. My gratitude also goes out to Michael Spooner, acquisitions editor at NCTE, and especially to Tim Bryant, NCTE publications staff, for his careful assistance with the manuscript. I am deeply indebted to Meredith Kopald and to Mona Johnson, my wife, for encouraging me in this project, for using ideas from these chapters in their classrooms, and for inspiring me with the results. Finally, my thanks goes out to all my writing students over the years.

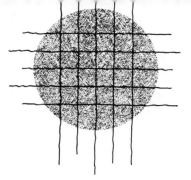

Word Weaving

Introduction

Word Weaving is about creativity and the poetic use of language. It is about the insider's approach to the imagination and creative writing. *Word Weaving* explains how poetry fits into our lives, how we create and mend the delicate web of relationships which makes human life both possible and desirable.

Word Weaving provides a program for writing and teaching poetry. It is *not* another "introduction to poetry" book which describes the nature of poetry, how to read and criticize it, and then how to write papers about it. Numerous other books take that approach.

Most literature courses in schools deal with works of poetry or fiction as finished products, and stress the analysis of them in discussion and papers. But literature is also a process, a way of looking at the world, a means of discovering various realities and their connections in and through language—a process of synthesizing. Art and poetry are human activities—verbs as well as nouns.

Analysis and Synthesis

Much of our education from childhood on is devoted to making distinctions between one thing and another, between fact and fantasy, thinking and feeling, stones and trees, male and female, success and failure, light and dark—on and on. The process of making clear distinctions and reducing a whole into its parts is an education in a particular kind of thinking, *analysis*. For many students—and, I dare say, for teachers as well—the world becomes so fragmented, so broken down into separate compartments and boxes with individual labels that, like Humpty Dumpty, it never quite gets back together again. A university education should conclude with a course called "Putting All the Pieces of the World Back Together Again."

Another kind of mental process, the opposite of analysis, is *synthesis*: the method of connecting parts into wholes, of relating wholes to other wholes and discovering overall unity. This has been called "holistic thinking." It involves linking body to mind, male to female, white skin to brown skin, country to city, art to science, Gilgamesh to John Wayne,

1

Egyptian pyramids to Mayan temples, Christianity to Buddhism, and all of these together.

Some observers maintain that we have become too analytical in the West, too preoccupied with parts and differences, resulting in a narrowed perception of reality, an overemphasis on the individual, and a loss of community. Lame Deer, a Sioux medicine man, comments:

> We have a saying that the white man sees so little, he must see with only one eye. We see a lot that you no longer notice . . . you are usually too busy. We Indians live in a world of symbols and images where the spiritual and the commonplace are one. To you symbols are just words, spoken or written in a book. To us they are part of nature, part of ourselves—the earth, the sun, the wind and the rain, stones, trees, animals, even little insects like ants and grasshoppers. We try to understand them not with the head but with the heart. (Lame Deer and Erdoes, 109)

In 1924 the psychologist Carl Jung traveled to the Southwest and visited the Taos pueblo in New Mexico, where he talked with Ochwiay Biano, the chief. Biano commented that white people are always seeking something: "The whites always want something; they are always uneasy and restless. We do not know what they want. We do not understand them." Jung then asked Biano why he thought this was true, and Biano answered, "They say that they think with their heads." And Jung said, "Why of course. What do you think with?" Pointing to his heart, the chief said, "We think here" (248).

"Thinking with the head" means analysis and the use of logic, data, and formulas—the realm of technology and science. "Thinking with the heart" involves synthesis and the feelings we have for our primary relationships. The *inside* member of a family with an appreciation of nuance and the inconspicuous has a different view of the family than the *outsider,* who knows only the broad strokes of physical appearances. Suppose now we extend the inside "family feeling" to embrace our neighbors, to the homeless downtown, to the fields and woods at the edge of town, and all the creatures living there. This is the essence of "thinking with the heart."

In Western history, the ascendancy of the sun, the development of rationalism and logic, the primacy of masculine deities, and the dominance of men over women are recognized by cultural historians as patriarchal characteristics. Goddess worship, the veneration of the moon, and the importance of intuition and imagination are associated with an earlier matriarchal or egalitarian society (see Eisler).

One could say that thinking with the head flowered in the Renaissance and prospered with the rise of science in the seventeenth, eighteenth and nineteenth centuries. Although we now live in the age of science and are persuaded by its products to worship in its pantheon, we have begun to realize the limitations of this cultural pattern. Thinking with the head and the patriarchal concerns need to be tempered and balanced by feminine values and thinking with the heart.

Public Language and Personal Language

In this book, the issue of relationship begins with language. The development of language by the first humans was undoubtedly instrumental in the birth of consciousness itself. Language has always been the prime tool and expression of mind and spirit. For the sake of preliminary sorting, it can be said that two basic roles for language have evolved.

The analytic process requires a *public* language: for dealing with our external reality; for describing, analyzing, and manipulating the objective world as something separate from ourselves; for shopping and banking; for giving orders or writing memos. As we approach the end of the twentieth century, the academic air buzzes with talk about returning to the basics. Schools need to teach the basic skills of literacy and computation, and provide a knowledge of history and science so that students can compete publicly in our modern world.

But the "basics" surely must also include the maturation of the inner person and the development of a second kind of language, a language of the heart: a *personal* language for emotions, for loved ones, for the neighbor and his dog next door, for meditation and prayer, for celebration and dreaming of a time when the lion will lie down with the lamb. These personal uses of language, called by Philip Wheelwright "depth language"(15), have traditionally been associated with literature, religion, and mythology, which serve as the vehicles for our most important psychological and spiritual relationships.

Religion and the arts have long provided for the twin poles of personal expression and community. We write to get in touch with the person inside, to melt down those icy prisons holding the self captive. At the same time, writing takes us into the world:

Why I Write

Touch:
    I strip the bark of things to feel them. I could touch faces.
    I wear my hair long for the feel on my back. I write with the
    feel of the paper. I could be blind.

Sight:
   Colors fly at me. I think I see people in the corner of my eye.
   There are designs in sugar spilt on the floor, in the folds of
   the paper I write on. I can't sleep until the stars on my
   ceiling stop glowing in the dark.

Smell:
   This is the sidewalk after rain. This is falling down. This is dirt
   in Rome. This is my grandmother's closet. This is Christmas.
   This is blood so thick it stops the breath.

Taste:
   My skin is salty. Blood is bitter. I love the image of a mouth.
   It burns, it gathers. A way to pull things to me: a sucking mouth.

Sound:
   I hear everything the same. I can hear a clock ticking, or
   someone talking to me, or a gunshot all at the same level of
   intensity. It isn't a bad thing. But I can't sleep if the heater
   hums or someone breathes beside me.

   —Kathy B./C*

Each of us has the capacity to re-create these images for ourselves, and slowly weave a web of relationships with other humans, plants, and animals. It is a delicate, tenuous web which needs constant care and regular repair to support us as human beings.

In my family's van, there is a handbook for medical emergencies on remote beaches or on camping trips in the mountains: what to do for hypothermia, sunstroke, broken limbs, blisters, and snakebites. *Word Weaving* is a kind of emergency handbook for modern victims of overexposure, poisons, anemia, loneliness, and dehydration—conditions which result from life in a pressure cooker, broken families, stress on the job, feelings of powerlessness, shifting identities, uncertainty about the future, plus overexposure to the media.

For all of the attractions of material existence and the pursuit of technological frontiers, it is imperative that human beings in the last years of the twentieth century confront the depths of the human psyche, explore the boundaries of consciousness, and rediscover the nurturing patterns of human community.

Contents and Organization of *Word Weaving*

This book is divided into two parts. The first part, "Poets and the Nature of Poetry," consists of chapters on the various roles of the poet, on the

*Note on student poetry and prose: With student writing I use the student's name plus his or her educational level at the time the piece was written, for example, Bruce D./JH. JH = junior high or middle school. HS = high school. C = college.

essential ingredients of poetry (image, metaphor, sound, and rhythm), and suggestions for the beginning writer.

Part II, "Weaving the World," contains eight chapters of writing topics, sample poems, suggestions for discussion and writing, and bibliography. Much of this material can be used in the classroom. If the first part of the text is seen as the head, dealing with some necessary background and theory, then the second part provides the heart, stomach, and limbs.

The format of part II is designed for beginning with oneself and then gradually moving outward by making connections with the world. The chapters are like a series of concentric circles radiating out from the center of consciousness, with the I (or eye, or Eye) in the middle. Beginning with the origins of the cosmos and the mysteries of birth, the chapters move through a series of relationships, such as family, friends, nature, and nation, outward to the heavens. The last chapter is on death and the mysteries of rebirth. The act of writing thus becomes a vehicle for the expansion of consciousness into the world.

My authorities and models are imaginative writers of all kinds from all ages. I often make use of mythology since it is the ancient repository of image, metaphor, and symbol—the foundation for poetry itself. In that place where myth, religion, poetry, drama, music, and dance meet, one can find the roots of the creative process and the training ground of the imagination. In learning about poetry and the creative process, I prefer to listen to insiders, rather than consult with outsiders like psychologists and critics who write *about* poets and poetry.

The Classroom

Most chapters in this text conclude with "Classroom Activities," a set of discussion questions and writing suggestions, open-ended in nature, that help students explore the sense and implications of the chapter's topics.

Different questions and exercises in the chapters will work with different age groups. Just as a young writer learns how to incorporate helpful suggestions into his or her writing, so a teacher soon learns about the capacity and competence of her or his class and can choose materials accordingly.

I encourage responses in kind: writing a poem is a splendid response to reading a poem. Obviously, writing a story or a play is also an appropriate response. One of the best-kept pedagogical secrets is that writing poems opens the door to reading and appreciating poems.

Unfortunately, some college English courses tend to condition students and future teachers to think that the most responsible and beneficial response to a piece of literature is an analytical or critical paper. The experience of reading literature, however, often calls forth images, memories, anecdotes, and associations from the past, which is a good reason for keeping a notebook or journal handy. A friend called these inner responses which float to the surface "uninvited images," and believed them to be a kind of gift from the buried parts of the psyche. Readers should be encouraged to value these materials, to nurture them within, and then express or re-create them in their own way.

Although *Word Weaving* is about poetry, the larger issues are self-expression and creating a human world for ourselves and others. When we choose language as a medium for this adventure, then we write. Some of that writing might end up as poems; some might be reflective or analytical. In the integrated curriculum, in the best of all possible classrooms, different kinds of writing would complement every phase of learning, since there is always an inside view and an outside view, a personal perspective and an objective perspective. A biology unit on the physiology of birth could also integrate writing about one's own beginnings and use poems by women about the birthing experience.

With literature and the creative process there are no ultimate theories or rules. Categories overlap and labels dissolve under scrutiny. I like Emily Dickinson's response: "If I read a book and it makes my whole body so cold no fire can ever warm me, I know that is poetry. If I feel physically as if the top of my head were taken off, I know that is poetry" (Johnson, 208).

My real faith is in self-expression and in a kind of anarchy of the imagination: that is, a situation where both teachers and students engage in the creative process, where each person becomes his or her own authority responsible for growth and maturity while actively participating in an energetic dialogue between internal and external realities.

When the Poems Are Gone

In the off season, I dream
of writing poems—some like
white birds, some like parrots.
Their wings in the long night feather
the air with mellifluous sounds.

The ones I covet most race along
the water like geese: their feet
slap the waves as they gain momentum,
their wings beat out tetrameters.
When they rise and soar, I stand

unsteadily in my unanchored boat.
Still landlocked, still adrift
without compass or paddle, I raise
my arms in salute as they fly by.
And I cheer.

—Charles Cockelreas

Identity and Creativity

In Polynesia there is a creation myth which begins with a solitary, primordial being:

> In the beginning Ta'aroa floated through space in an egg-like shell, before any of the world had been created, before sun and moon, before plants and animals. Ta'aroa tapped at the shell until finally it broke.
> Stepping out onto the shell, he cried out, "Who is above there? Who is below there?" There was no answer. "Who is in front there? Who is in back there?" Again, no answer. Only the echo of his voice bouncing in space and nothing more.
> Then Ta'aroa ordered, "O rock, crawl over here!" But there was no rock to obey him. So he ordered, "O sand, crawl over here!" But there was no sand to obey him. Then Ta'aroa became very upset because he was not obeyed and he thought about what he would do next. (retold from Long, 141)

In this story about the beginnings of the cosmos is a vivid portrait of the birth of consciousness in each individual, an emerging from one's shell and an awakening to the outside world. Initially this awakening occurs when we are babies, but in different forms it becomes part of all the stages of growing up and growing old. We grow, we change, we withdraw, we reach out, we change, and so on. And with each stage we must rediscover who we are.

The seeds of creativity are buried in questions of identity, location, and relationship. It is frightening to ask for a response from the world, as Ta'aroa did, and hear nothing but silence. One basic reason for creativity is this feeling of isolation, and the need to reach out to other beings. Ta'aroa's remedy for his solitary condition was to create the world:

> Half of the shell, from which he emerged, was raised to make the sky. The other half became the rock and sand of earth. He took his own spine for mountain ranges, his ribs became mountain slopes. He took his lungs for large, billowing clouds, his flesh for the fatness of the earth, his arms and legs for power in the earth. His finger nails and toe nails were changed into scales and shells for fishes, his feathers into trees, shrubs and grasses to clothe the

earth, his intestines into lobsters, shrimp and eels for the rivers
and seas. The blood of Ta'aroa became heated and floated away,
becoming the redness of the sky and the redness of rainbows.
(retold from Long, 141)

In many cultures there is a deity or primordial being who provides
a model for mortals by creating the world out of him- or herself—by
dismemberment. In imitation of this first creation, it is up to each of
us to re-create a livable world out of our own inner resources, to
remember (re-member) ourselves, to use imagination and memory to
create a whole life in which psyche, family, ancestors, race, and species
are connected.

Weaving and Spinning

A Sioux legend tells about an old woman who sits in the moonlight
weaving the tapestry of the world with porcupine quills. Nearby a kettle
of herbs is boiling over a fire. A dog watches her. Occasionally she leaves
her work and stirs the herbs. Then the dog gets up, goes over to her
weaving, and unravels it. Returning to the tapestry, she begins again.
This has been going on for thousands of years. If she ever completed
her work it would mean the end of the world (*Legends*, 105).

In one form or another this image of the woman weaving together
reality is repeated throughout the world. Sometimes it is the spider
woman (or Cosmic Spider) who creates the web of life out of her own
body, and connects all the various parts of nature with her delicate
threads. The spider's web is a microcosm of the unity of the world.

All the mother goddesses of the ancient world were spinners and
weavers, and thus weaving became a marvelous metaphor for creativity
and synthesis, the process of creating a world web. The thread of the
Great Weaver is the umbilical cord which attaches each individual to
the creator as well as to the world tapestry into which each destiny is
woven.

Symbolically, the warp of the tapestry represents the vertical plane:
our transcendent concerns, the spiritual dimension, the eternal forms
and timeless principles. The weft or woof represents the horizontal
plane: the day-to-day existence of things in time and space, the material
dimension. Each crossing of the warp and woof symbolizes a coming-
together of two dimensions and the reconciliation of opposites: the joining of spirit and matter, day and night, male and female.

The idea of weaving suggests pattern—that the universe has design
and purpose, that the various parts fit into a whole. It is up to the
individual artist to discover these patterns and to weave his or her own

particular visions into the larger design of the whole. The weaving itself creates, sustains, and harmonizes.

Closely related to weaving is the spinner, who transforms raw wool into yarn or thread and winds it on a spool. Spinners are the Norns or Fates whose scissors determine the length of each lifetime, while the weaver determines the fabric within which each life is temporally suspended.

Spinning and weaving have an internal reference as well:

> The first time I tried to spin I found it almost impossible to coordinate the rotation of the wheel with my foot and the twisting and feeding onto the bobbin of the wool I was attempting to spin. It was like trying to do two incompatible things at once. Gradually, I was able to harmonize the two until now spinning is a form of meditation for me in that I am able to "untangle the knots" of my daily routine just by sitting down and spinning for awhile. It awakens a center within me that is rich in imagery—it is almost like the twilight state of awareness before falling asleep.

> —Sue S./C

The weaving metaphor applies to all of the arts, but in this book it is particularly appropriate to writing, to poetry. The writer, like the spider at the center of her own creativity, spins a web of relationships, attaching one image to another, a butterfly to a rock, an ancestor to a neighborhood, a crisis to a labyrinth—from inside to outside, and back again.

The final goal of creative writing is to create a community of the living, an inclusive community which, bit by bit, being by being, expands into a global perspective. It shares these functions with all of the other arts, with mythology, religion, music, and drama. Spiritual extremes are woven together in "The Song of the Sky Loom," from the Pueblo Indians of the Southwest:

> O our Mother the Earth, O our Father the Sky,
> Your children are we, and with tired backs
> We bring you the gifts you love.
> Then weave for us a garment of brightness;
> May the warp be the white light of morning,
> May the weft be the red light of evening,
> May the fringes be the falling rain,
> May the border be the standing rainbow.
> Thus weave for us a garment of brightness,
> That we may walk fittingly where birds sing,
> That we may walk fittingly where grass is green,
> O our Mother the Earth, O our Father the Sky.

> (Spinden, 94)

References

Eisler, Riane. 1988. *The Chalice and the Blade: Our History, Our Future.* San Francisco: Harper & Row.

Johnson, Thomas H., ed. 1971. *Emily Dickinson: Selected Letters.* Cambridge: Harvard University Press.

Jung, Carl. 1961. *Memories, Dreams, Reflections.* Edited by Aniela Jaffé. New York: Vintage Books.

Lame Deer, John Fire, and Richard Erdoes. 1972. *Lame Deer: Seeker of Visions.* New York: Simon and Schuster.

Legends of the Mighty Sioux. 1960 [1941]. Compiled by Workers of the South Dakota Writers' Project, Work Projects Administration. Sioux Falls, S.D.: Fantab, Inc.

Long, Charles H. 1963. *Alpha: The Myths of Creation.* New York: George Braziller.

Spinden, Herbert J., trans. 1933. *Songs of the Tewa.* New York: Exposition of Indian Tribal Arts, Inc.

Wheelwright, Philip. 1968. *The Burning Fountain: A Study in the Language of Symbolism.* New and revised ed. Bloomington, Ind.: Indiana University Press.

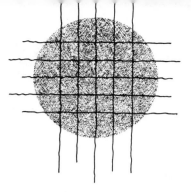

I Poets and
the Nature of Poetry

1 Voices of the Poet

To create poetry is as natural as breathing. Poetry and breathing have an essential connection:

> In Eskimo, the word "to make poetry" is the word "to breathe"; both are derivatives of *anerca*—the soul which is eternal: the breath of life. A poem is words infused with breath or spirit: "Let me breathe of it," says the poet-maker and then begins: "I have put my poem in order on the threshold of my tongue." (Carpenter, 51)

The Latin root of *inspiration* involves breathing, a reminder that creating is as common and essential as breathing.

In the Hebrew tradition the ultimate model for this creative process is found in Genesis when Yahweh breathes life into the first humans—breath as the divine ingredient of life itself. For the artist, "divine inspiration" contains the idea of "being breathed by God."

The transcendent source of creativity was attributed by the early Greek poets to the Muses—nine goddesses who presided over the arts—with the implication that although creativity might be as natural as breathing, its ultimate source is a mystery. Poems or parts of poems seem to "come" to the poet from an unknown place in the psyche; in that sense, the poet seems to be a medium for the poem, as if the poem were being written through the agency of the poet.

The possibilities for creating poetry are as various, natural, and mysterious as life itself. Before attending to more formal definitions and descriptions of poetry (see chapters 2 and 3), we will briefly explore in this chapter the variety of roles that poets have discovered for themselves: as singers, storytellers, name-givers, magicians, explorers, and insiders.

Singer

One of the oldest roles for the poet is that of singer. Some linguists believe that song was the earliest form of speech; certainly song ranks as a very early use of language. A legend from Estonia points to the

13

primordial importance of song, and reveals the human capacity to not
only appreciate nature's songs but also to express the depths and heights
of our experiences:

> The god of song, Wannemunne, once descended onto the
> Domberg, and there, in a sacred wood, played and sang music of
> divine beauty. All creatures were invited to listen, and they each
> learned some fragment of the celestial sound: the forest learned
> its rustling, the stream its roar; the wind caught and learned to
> re-echo the shrillest tones, and the birds the prelude of the song.
> The fishes stuck their heads as far as the eyes out of the water, but
> left their ears below the surface; they saw the movements of the
> god's mouth and imitated them, but remained dumb. Man alone
> grasped it all, and therefore his song pierces into the depths of the
> heart, and mounts upward to the dwellings of the gods. (retold in
> Wheelwright, 3)

One dimension of song is spontaneity: humans sing when they are
happy or sad, confident or fearful. We say they "burst into song." Many
aspiring troubadours rehearse in the shower while soaping down. Full
hearts naturally sing, or sing naturally. Orpingalik, an Eskimo, explains
about the psychological conditions for creating a new song:

> Songs are thoughts, sung out with the breath when people are
> moved by great forces and ordinary speech no longer suffices. Man
> moved just like the ice floe sailing here and there out in the cur-
> rent. His thoughts are driven by a flowing force when he feels joy,
> when he feels sorrow. Thoughts can wash over him like a flood,
> making his blood come in gasps and his heart throb. . . . When the
> words we want to use shoot up of themselves—we get a new song.
> (Carpenter, 51)

I wrote down two of my daughter Sarah's songs when she was four-
and-a-half years old and sang to her five-month-old sister, Maia. She
plunked a broken plastic ukulele and created her songs by leafing
through picture books. After each song she circled Maia, blowing a
plastic harmonica. The use of "Oh yah" is effective rhythmically. With
the last two lines of the second song she captures a small miracle of
maturation.

Sarah's Songs

I. Oh the lizard, the blue lizard
   Oh yah
   Meets a lizard on another page
   Oh yah
   They're on a big rock
   They're on the road
   Oh yah
   On the road, on their way to town
   Oh yah

II. Oh Herod, King Herod was terrible,
Oh Herod was a terrible man.
He killed the children
All the children, oh yah.

And Baby Jesus, oh Baby Jesus
Went to Egypt, oh yah
Went to Egypt far from Herod.
He saw the pyramids in the desert
and became a boy, oh yah.

—Sarah Johnson

Early humans used song for practical purposes: hunting songs, planting and harvesting songs. Hymns, chants, and prayers are poetic forms suitable for relationships with the unseen, mysterious powers that run the universe. But always the love song has been important.

The oldest written love song comes from Sumer over 4,000 years ago. It was probably used in a sacred marriage rite between the king and a priestess to ensure the land's fertility. In this excerpt, the bride-priestess is speaking:

Bridegroom, let me caress you,
My precious caress is more savory than honey,
In the bedchamber, honey filled,
Let us enjoy your goodly beauty,
Lion, let me caress you,
My precious caress is more savory than honey.

(Kramer, 213)

These lines remind us that the mysteries of union and birth involve sensuality as well as religious ritual.

After humans developed a personal relationship with their god or gods, religion and sensuality easily became entwined in the language of love. Because of these connections, there have been varying interpretations of "The Song of Songs" in the Bible, ranging from a couple in love to the wooing of Israel by God (Yahweh). In this excerpt spoken by the bride, the nature imagery is very suggestive:

I hear my Beloved.
See how he comes
leaping on the mountains,
bounding over the hills.
My Beloved is like a gazelle,
like a young stag.

See where he stands
behind our wall.
He looks in at the window,
he peers through the lattice.

My Beloved lifts up his voice,
he says to me,
"Come then, my love,
my lovely one, come.
For see, winter is past,
the rains are over and gone.
The flowers appear on the earth.
The season of glad songs has come,
the cooing of the turtledove is heard
in our land.
The fig tree is forming its first figs
and the blossoming vines give out their fragrance.
Come then, my love,
my lovely one, come.
My dove, hiding in the clefts of the rock,
in the coverts of the cliff,
show me your face,
let me hear your voice;
for your voice is sweet
and your face is beautiful."

(Song of Songs 2:8–14, *Jerusalem Bible*)

The male is compared to a virile animal, a gazelle or stag; the female
is compared to fertile nature or a turtledove, often a symbol of sexual
passion. But the crux of this passage is in the pleading of the man for
a glimpse of the woman and a few words from her. A similar situation
exists for the young songster with his guitar who serenades his true
love under her bedroom window.

Today the most popular kind of song is still the love song, with its
three basic themes: (1) Please look at me, I'm starving for love! (2) Now
that someone loves me, I'm on top of the world! and (3) Why, oh why
did you leave me? I feel like dying!

Whitman reminds us of various songs when he equates the energetic
work of building America with singing in "I Hear America Singing":

I hear America singing, the varied carols I hear,
Those of mechanics, each one singing his as it should be blithe
    and strong,
The carpenter singing his as he measures his plank or beam,
The mason singing his as he makes ready for work, or leaves off
    work,
The boatman singing what belongs to him in his boat, the deck-
    hand singing on the steamboat deck,
The shoemaker singing as he sits on his bench, the hatter singing
    as he stands,
The wood-cutter's song, the ploughboy's on his way in the morn-
    ing, or at noon intermission or at sundown,

The delicious singing of the mother, or of the young wife at work,
  or of the girl sewing or washing,
Each singing what belongs to him or her and to none else, . . .

Storyteller

Song and story are the twin poles of poetry. But note that we are using
the word *story* in a special way: not story as fiction—something made
up or untrue—but story as those events which are part of one's own
history. Imaginative narrative, but *not* imaginary narrative.

The storytelling role stretches back to a time when poets were bards,
skalds, or minstrels—a time prior to the written word. They were a kind
of vocal newspaper earning their living by wandering from village to
village with the latest gossip. The storyteller was also the tribal historian,
a person who memorized the tribe's stories, from creation to the present.

A Papago Indian of Arizona told Ruth Underhill about the role of the
father in storytelling:

> On winter nights, when we had finished our gruel or rabbit stew
> and lay back on our mats, my brother would say to my father: "My
> father, tell us something."
> My father would lie quietly upon his mat with my mother beside
> him and the baby between them. At last he would start slowly to
> tell us about how the world began. This is a story that can be told
> only in winter when there are no snakes about, for if the snakes
> heard they would crawl in and bite you. But in winter when the
> snakes are asleep, we tell these things. Our story about the world
> is full of songs, and when the neighbors heard my father singing
> they would open our door and step in over the high threshold.
> Family by family they came, and we made a big fire and kept the
> door shut against the cold night. When my father finished a
> sentence we would all say the last word after him. If anyone went
> to sleep he would stop. He would not speak anymore. But we did
> not go to sleep. (199)

Homer provided literary immortality for the Greek heroes of the
Trojan War. Virgil celebrated Aeneas and his followers. Dante immor-
talized a number of Florentine citizens of the Middle Ages. Every age
and culture has its storytellers. The bards and minstrels of the United
States stretch from Walt Whitman to Woody Guthrie to Joan Baez,
Odetta, Bob Dylan, and Bruce Springsteen. But my question then is,
who is singing *your* particular history into existence? Who is imaging
you, telling your story? If you do not live in a tribe with its storytellers,
it is probable that no one is telling your story or your family's. In fact,
it might be necessary for you to become the storyteller.

Our culture is changing so rapidly that many stories of the past generations—immigrating from a foreign country, arriving broke in the United States, homesteading in the West, stories of hardship and survival during the Depression, and many others—will be lost. Some ethnic groups, such as the Irish and the Chicanos, have preserved the importance of storytelling. The Navajo Indians in the Southwest have a saying, "Knowing a good story will protect your home, children and property" (Kluckhohn and Leighton, 234). Other immigrant groups believed, sadly enough, that old-country ethnic stories were to be replaced by American stories, just as the foreign tongue was to be exchanged for English.

Our consciousness was changed permanently by the television series based on Alex Haley's book *Roots:* having roots was good, a source of pride. Tracing one's roots became important. Without roots the tree cannot stand straight and tall.

A student in a writing class said that it was so very sad that her grandfather in California had died before he had a chance to tell his story. Other students have said that they were sorry that their grandparents had not left some kind of written record about their lives. The genealogical data of family trees or charts was a start, but they wanted personal stories about childhood, growing up, getting married, going to work, having fun on holidays, victories and defeats.

Collecting becomes part of storytelling: stories on tape recorders, family histories, old letters, clippings from newspapers, notebooks and journals. One father collected a piece of his son's history in a poem:

Baseball

Son, there are words that send
runners rounding third all the way home
and words
of encouragement   when you're alone
    and distressed on the pitcher's mound
I share the tenseness you try to hide
    behind your Little League face
I share
    and in the bottom of the last inning
with bases loaded, two out, winning run on third,
You, my son, at the plate
    alone with the bat and your near-perfect stance
(I whisper from the dugout I love you
no matter what   ball or strike   hit or miss
                I love you)

Your base hit into the gap in right center
   clears the bases
   clears the stands
Your teammates swallow you
   with true jubilation
I stand aside. Hugging you without touching.

                    —Roy Ricci

In our affluent society, most important events, such as marriages and birthdays, are attended by cameras; why not also make sure a poet or tribal historian is present to record the event in language?

Magician, Priest, and Name-Giver

Names are so important! We make contact with the things of this world through names. We gain some control through names: a person can be called, summoned, chastised, or praised through his or her name. Our first ancestor, Adam, learned about the process of naming:

> So from the soil Yahweh God fashioned all the wild beasts and all the birds of heaven. These he brought to the man to see what he would call them; each one was to bear the name the man would give it. The man gave names to all the cattle, all the birds of heaven and all the wild beasts. (Genesis 2: 19–20, *Jerusalem Bible*)

Imagine a large creature with a swaying trunk slowly approaching Adam and then waiting patiently for a name. Adam scratches his head, wrinkles his forehead, and then with a bit of inspiration he says, "Elephant." Of course Adam was right every time: he gave each creature its right name, the name that belonged to that species. I think of Adam as the Bible's first poet.

In ancient cultures the person who collected and manipulated the power names, the names for gods and goddesses, was the magician or priest. "Abracadabra" is one of the most widely used magical incantations; it has a long history of popularity and use, dating back as far as the Roman Empire. When used for healing, it was written on a piece of paper, which was hung around the patient's neck for nine days, then thrown over the shoulder into a stream flowing to the east. The idea was that as the letters of the phrase dwindled to nothing, so the fever would shrink away. In a section from his "Candul," a young poet captures the flavor of the arcane, the mystical, and the religio-magical role of the poet:

Galileo,

Agrippa,

Copernicus,
Paracelsus,
hinting at archetypes we fear but do not find in
Jung or even the Cabala.
Withering spells,
Heavy smoke,
Thick-ground lenses.
Under German roofs, Italian vaults,
arcana of the Spiritus Mundi.
Damp,
dessicant,
dead
dust in pyramids,
ziggurats groveling before Oriental constellations.
Images,
   symbols,
      talismans
a/g/a/i/n/s/t/ the inner presence or o u t e r
     c h a o s
Sands of e te rni tyb lowing over the dead (deaderthan-
   Ozymandias)

               m r c
Faces of Ur— faces which   like arms the oceans
             e b a e
and
             t e h
deserts of the world in their
          e t

—Robert M./HS

Children go through stages where they repeatedly ask for the names of things they see: "What is that?" "What is this?" To know is to name. When my daughter Maia learned the name "Da-da" at about fourteen months she also tried a bit of word magic; she said "Da-da" and expected me to appear. I wrote a little poem:

> Maia says Da-da Da-da
> all day, from every room
> behind, beside, in front
> of me.

> With each word
> I slowly inflate
> until I am a giant
> dancing on the roof.

Often we have very strong convictions about whether a name fits a person or object, whether the name is suitable. Samuel Butler said that the true test of imagination was finding a fitting name for a cat. The official bureau of name-giving does not always equal Adam's imagination. The name "Pikes Peak," for example, does not seem to measure up to the majesty and size of this mountain outside of Colorado Springs, Colorado. Zebulon Pike might have been the first white man to explore the base of the mountain, but he certainly did not discover it, nor did he even get to the top of it. What do you suppose was that mountain's original name?

John Steinbeck, however, describes a name which is a perfect fit:

> In geographic naming it seems almost as though the place contributed something to its own name.... It doesn't matter what California means; what does matter is that with the names bestowed upon this place, "California" has seemed right to those who have seen it. And the meaningless word "California" has completely routed all the "New Albions" and "Carolinas" from the scene. (55)

How many of the following names seem to fit: ant, potato, wasp, hawk, meat, lettuce, blood? *Wasp* is particularly good, isn't it? Sometimes the word in another language works better with my ear: the Spanish *sangre* has more throbbing life than *blood;* the Spanish *fresa* seems more delicious than *strawberry.*

As our society becomes more technological, reducing people and events to statistics, some of the magic nevertheless remains with personal names:

I Think I Remember How

I whisper your name to the moon
   and stretch my arms out toward the stars
Choose one and make a wish that
    somehow   somewhere
you could touch my fingertips
and echo back my cries

—M. A./HS

(See chapter 5 for more discussion of names and naming.)

Explorer and Insider

A coyote story from the Montana Salish tribe illustrates the importance of the explorer role and the imagination required of the insider.

One day while Coyote is out for a walk, he is warned by a bird that the next valley ahead is really a dragon which will swallow him. Coyote cuts down a tamarack tree to prevent his being swallowed and proceeds on his journey. When asked by a disembodied voice why he is carrying the tree, Coyote finds out that he has already been swallowed:

> Surprised and worried, Coyote looked around him and saw only bones on the ground. Over by a tree was the person speaking to him—just recently swallowed and already thin as a shadow. He told Coyote that there was nothing to eat, but Coyote looked around and saw big pieces of fat hanging down from above. Pulling out his magic flint knife, he cut away some fat, and when he did so, a large glob overhead began to move back and forth in spasms of pain.
>
> "That must be the dragon's heart!" Coyote said. "Now I know how to kill her." In a loud voice Coyote spoke to everyone in the stomach, to the bones of the dead and the shadows of the living: "Get ready to escape," he shouted. "After I cut the dragon's heart and it falls, run as fast as you can to get out of this valley before the dragon's openings close!"
>
> Standing on his tall tamarack tree, Coyote used his flint knife to cut away at the dragon's heart. The moment it dropped, all the dead animals came alive and, with the rest of the victims, ran for the openings. Some escaped through the mouth, others like Coyote fled through the tail.
>
> The ones who escaped first, when the openings were large, became the big animals—buffalo, moose and grizzly bear. As the openings grew smaller, so did the size of the animals, until the last ones out, the little wood ticks, had to flatten themselves to escape just before the opening closed.
>
> As the animals gathered around Coyote to thank him, he gave each of them names. He named Eagle, the highest flyer and sky hunter. He named Bear, for strength and endurance. He named Owl for big medicine and extra sight, Sturgeon for the largest fish in the river, and Salmon for the best tasting fish. And then he named himself: "I am Coyote, the wisest and smartest of all the animals."
> (retold from Miller and Harrison, 20–24)

In North American Indian stories, Coyote is often a trickster figure who is adept at survival and knows the secrets of renewal. In the story above, he also provides us with a fine model for a workaday poet and for the creative process.

First, he takes a risk. He knows that going ahead with his life could be dangerous, but he proceeds anyway, hungry, curious, a bit nosey. He must deal with the dragon of reality, for his benefit and the safety of others.

Next, he prepares himself and then goes to the heart of the matter in the dragon's belly, which is comparable to Jonah's rebirth experience in the belly of the whale. Others before him got swallowed by their lives, by their fears, and are slowly starving and withering away.

The situation looks impossible, but he doesn't give up; he attends to his hunger and thereby discovers the vulnerable organ. With a bit of ingenuity, a mythic tool, and a grandiose announcement to the living and the dead, he frees the heart and provides an escape from captivity. Life is reborn.

Lastly, he gives identity to himself and his fellow creatures with names, since purpose and meaning flow out of the proper name. And in a moment of vaingloriousness, he is proud of his accomplishments.

I think of Coyote as a poet who combines audacity and mythic craft with language in order to descend into life's dark underbelly and return to re-create new perimeters of health and freedom. He is the legendary *insider*, as well as an explorer. Many creative people of all kinds have explored the repressed sides of human nature in order to bring some bit of creation to light. Both the Romantic poets and the French symbolists became famous for venturing into the murky waters of the psyche, often risking sanity in the exploration of new psychological territory.

Since World War II, various social and ethnic minorities have in turn become explorers of the dragon's belly, exposing to the dominant class ever-more-threatening dimensions of reality: women, Native Americans, Hispanics, blacks, Chinese, gays, senior citizens, abused children, veterans, and others.

The high school student who wrote the following untitled poem asked to remain anonymous. She is a gifted explorer and insider.

> Mental illness
> In a family.
> A shy boy, tall, shy boy.
> Artist, excellent one.
> Intelligent.
> Flunking school.
>
> Psychiatrists, therapy.
> A mother.
> Commitment,
> Devoting her time, devoting her soul
> To a boy who is frightened,
> Will not leave the house.
> Steadfast suffering
> Because he has no one else.
>
> A father.
> Anger,
> Because he'd worked hard at his life,
> Been honest, done what was right.

Confusion,
Because his son should have been like him,
Because suicide scares us all
When it is so probable.

A sister.
Immaturity.
Self-pity,
Because this is exciting to her.
Guilt,
Because she conveniently has the bathroom to herself
While her brother struggles in a mental ward.
Fear,
Because this disease is genetic;
Her children might have it,
She can develop it.
Loneliness,
Because societal prejudice
Might hurt him extremely.
He may be her responsibility someday.
Friends do not understand.
Parents cannot understand.
Scott will never
Understand.

And love.
Deep, stinging love
For a brother.
A brother I had seen
And never seen,
Grown up with,
Never known.
Loved . . .
Without comprehending
The meaning of love.

Classroom Activities

Discussion Questions

1. Everyone has a song to sing, a story to tell. What prevents people from singing their songs and telling their stories?
2. What role or roles do the singing poets who fill our airwaves play in our society?
3. Are there additional roles that poets play in modern society?
4. Do you know any magical names or charms?
5. How would you modernize the Coyote story? What is analogous to the dragon's belly? What is a modern version of Coyote's knife?

Writing Suggestions

1. Are there members of your family who are singers or storytellers? Write about one of them.
2. Are there TV commercials with "magical" sayings? Make a list of them. Pretend that you are a modern magician and try them out.
3. Write about the most powerful names that you know.
4. When we write about inner feelings, we are using language to explore the world within. Make a list of the areas within that need exploration.

References

Carpenter, Edmund. 1973. *Eskimo Realities*. New York: Holt, Rinehart and Winston.

Jones, Alexander, ed. 1966. *Jerusalem Bible*. Garden City, N.Y.: Doubleday & Co.

Kluckhohn, Clyde, and Dorothea Leighton. 1962. *The Navaho*. New York: Doubleday and Co.

Kramer, Samuel Noah. 1959. *History Begins at Sumer*. New York: Doubleday Anchor Books.

Miller, Harriet, and Elizabeth Harrison. n.d. *Coyote Tales of the Montana Salish*. Browning, Mont.: Museum of the Plains Indian.

Steinbeck, John. 1952. *The Log from the Sea of Cortez*. New York: Random House.

Underhill, Ruth Murray. *The Autobiography of a Papago Woman* (AAA Memoirs, 1936); quoted in Margot Astrov, *American Indian Prose and Poetry*. 1962. New York: Capricorn Books.

Wheelwright, Philip. 1968. *The Burning Fountain: A Study in the Language of Symbolism*. New and revised ed. Bloomington, Ind.: Indiana University Press.

Whitman, Walt. 1973. *Leaves of Grass*. Edited by Sculley Bradley and Harold W. Blodgett. New York: W. W. Norton & Co.

2 The Nature of Poetry

When we view a poem as a finished product, it is tempting to conclude that the basic ingredients of poetry, such as metaphor and meter, have been added to ordinary language to raise it to the level of poetry, like adding candles and frosting to a cake. This analytic view regards the language of poetry as *ornamentation*. Reading and analyzing the poem involves reducing it to its constituent parts and appreciating how they combine to create the poem's meaning.

An alternative view regards poetic language as a means of exploring both the inner world of the person and the phenomenal world outside, and of creating imaginative relationships with these worlds.

On the one hand, poetic devices and patterns may be designated or fixed, and be passed down from one generation to another as literary conventions—that is, *closed forms*. On the other hand, the poetic forms may be new for each poem, created as a reflection of the content of the poem—*open forms*.

It is important to remember throughout this discussion that poems have an "organic" unity, which simply means that a poem, like a living thing, has a vitality and significance that transcends a description and categorization of its parts. After all the analysis has been made, there will always be something more about a good poem or painting or piece of music that cannot be explained.

A number of introductions to poetry thoroughly define, explain, and illustrate figures of speech, metrical structure, and conventional poetic forms. Two excellent books are Paul Fussell's *Poetic Meter and Poetic Form* and Lewis Turco's *The New Book of Forms: A Handbook of Poetics*. There is no need to duplicate that information here.

Definitions and Ornamentation

Historically, it was thought that poetry was distinguished from prose in two general ways: (1) a poem has a larger, more concentrated dose of poetic elements, such as imagery, metaphor, meter, and alliteration; and (2) a poem *looks* like poetry, with shorter lines and regular stanzas.

An image is usually defined as a sensory description of objects in a poem; images are often visual representations, but they can involve any of the senses. A "figure of speech" is defined here by a standard literary handbook:

> Intentional departure from the normal order, construction, or meaning of words in order to gain strength and freshness of expression, to create a pictorial effect, to describe by ANALOGY, or discover and illustrate similarities in otherwise dissimilar things. (Thrall, Hibbard, and Holman, 202)

Following this is a list of the more common figures of speech: antithesis, apostrophe, climax, hyperbole, irony, metaphor, metonymy, personification, simile, and synecdoche.

The assumption behind the above definition is that figures of speech are things which are added to normal language in order to elevate it to poetry: they are ornaments or table dressing. In this regard they are like conventional meters which are also added on to make "poetry." Alexander Pope captures this view in a couplet from the eighteenth century:

> True wit is Nature to advantage dressed;
> What oft was thought, but ne'er so well expressed.

Using this perspective, one would view the process of writing a poem as something like this: the poet has an idea for a poem, which is then translated into language. Poetic devices such as allusion, paradox, and meter are added in order to make the poem more poetic, that is, more musical and more complex. The task of the student reader, often under the tutelage of a teacher, is to reverse this process by dissecting the poem into its parts, by penetrating the obscure layers of metaphorical and metrical meaning to arrive at the original thought or perception.

This model seems appropriate for certain poets and historical periods, such as English poetry prior to 1800, but when we consider all periods of poetry around the world, there are too many varieties of poems to include under a single umbrella. Samuel Johnson, the famous eighteenth-century lexicographer and critic, responded to an inquiry about poetry by responding, "Why, Sir, it is much easier to say what it is not. We all know what light is; but it is not easy to *tell* what it is" (Boswell, 744).

Although many poems still look like conventional poems today, the line between poetry and prose, between poetry and graphics, between poetry and drama, can be fuzzy. For the time being, it is simply easier to accept the designation of the person who wrote a particular piece, or the editor's word, for what appears in a literary journal or book: if a piece of writing is called a poem, I accept that. We will leave exact definitions to the academics and critics who make their living with such matters.

From the point of view of the creative process, the basic ingredients of poetry involve not component parts but *relationships*, that is, connections with the outer world and the inner world.

Image: Connecting with the Outer World

Ezra Pound uses a charming story to illustrate the idea that the language of poetry is the language of exploration:

> I once saw a small child go to an electric light switch and say, "Mamma, can I *open* the light?" She was using the age-old language of exploration, the language of art. It was a sort of metaphor, but she was not using it as ornamentation. (36)

Images provide a medium for participating in the world: seeing, hearing, smelling, touching, tasting. Images allow us to envision the world, hear its voices, smell roasting corn and cotton candy at the state fair. Images excite the imagination ("image-ination"), and via the imagination we attend to the physical world—in our mind's eye we can see and hear the activities of the night:

> Night, Night
>
> green moon
> edging in
> over the black
>
> poplars
>
> worms
> digging freeways
> under
> the sunflowers
>
> —Jeanne Shannon

Images provide our basic contact with the world.

Image: Connecting with the Inner World

For reasons that are not clear, images can be a bridge into the deeper contents of the psyche when rational or logical thought is stopped at the border. How often an image in a piece of literature calls forth a flood of emotion from deep inside the unconscious, and the reader feels overwhelmed by past associations and memories!

Advertising companies, public relations firms, and political campaign operatives are well aware of the power of images. With young writers, however, it is often necessary to encourage them to stick with the image and avoid drifting into abstractions and explanations.

A rough rule of thumb for both the writer and the reader is this: an image keeps the participant close to the experience of the poem; ideas and abstractions cause the reader or writer to think *about* the experience and to therefore step back from it. *The creative process is the process of giving birth to images, whether it is the writer imaging the darkness within or the reader responding from a similar depth to the images in a poem.*

A strange power emanates from a poem carefully hewn from images, as if inner and outer become one:

> A sudden gray-rock stillness comes
> before snow falls
> . . . the sky an opened oyster
> slips dark pearl
>
> Crystalizing, the universe
> shards
> a cold, thin sound
> piercing the spirit.
>
> —Dorrit O./C

A good image reverberates, as if it were reaching out to make connections with other images, places, and times. Almost unavoidably the poetic image shifts into metaphor, and inanimate objects come alive:

> Junk-Yard
>
> Tires, treadless, lying
>   sleeping
> on exposed torsos
>   revealing their tired feet
>   calloused
> they're scattered in the midst
>   of doors
> reluctantly ripped from their hinges
>   and windshields
> cracked   teenaged
>   in some friday night
>   screaming down the road
>
> —Jay U./C

Certain images seem to strike responsive chords within, often at the very fringes of understanding, as if an ancient symbol were re-created in modern dress:

snakes

snakes are coming down the mountains
snakes like long rocks not yet calcified
not yet converted to maple tree limbs
in a city park, ignorant snakes
who don't know the age of reptiles has passed
snakes, you can see them if you lie sideways
their scales reflected in your aluminum beer can

snakes are walking into town
innocent, not knowing what their new shapes will be
and, like snakes, not wanting to ask.

—Joseph Somoza

Behind this poem are the serpentine shapes of nature and the capacity
of the snake to shed its skin and renew itself—a traditional symbol of
healing and immortality for peoples around the world.

Today people in the holistic health field realize what traditional
peoples have always known: that imaging is a way of dealing with
disease. The anthropologist Barre Toelken personally experienced the
connection between imaging and healing while living on the Navajo
reservation in Arizona. He became ill, perhaps with pneumonia, and
it was thought he could be cured by the Red Ant Ceremony:

> A medicine man (in Navajo, literally a "singer") was sent for who
> knew the ceremony, and I was later advised I was being treated
> for red ants in my system which I had no doubt picked up by
> urinating on an ant hill. Some time after the ritual, which was quite
> successful . . . I had occasion to discuss the treatment with the singer:
> had I really had ants in my system, did he think? His answer was
> a hesitant "no, not ants, but Ants" (my capitalization, to indicate
> the gist of his remark). Finally, he said, "We have to have a way
> of thinking strongly about disease." (231)

The image provides a means of locating the disease so that the powers
of the psyche can focus on healing. It is not clear how an image can
penetrate ordinary consciousness, but an image is a way of "thinking
strongly" about both health and disease, inner realities and outer
realities.

Imagine the potential power of the poetic image for good or ill. *The
image is the heart of poetry.*

Metaphor: The Warp and Woof of Relationships

The broadest use of the word *metaphor* ties it to the underlying interconnectedness of reality. In order to appreciate this meaning of

metaphor, it is helpful to return briefly to the Polynesian story of Ta'aroa, who in his solitude created a world out of his body: his spine became mountains, his lungs clouds, his fingernails shells, and so forth (see "Introduction," above). From this story we can grasp the metaphorical nature of reality: that the human body is a primary agent of metaphor and is analogous to the rest of nature. We fit in, we are related, because we share these connections. The story concludes with a commentary:

> As Ta'aroa had shells, so has everything a shell. The sky is a shell: that is, endless space in which the gods placed the sun, the moon, the Sporades, and the constellations of the gods.
> The earth is a shell to the stones, the water, and plants that spring from it.
> Man's shell is woman because it is by her that he comes into the world; and woman's shell is woman because she is born of woman.
> One cannot enumerate the shells of all the things that this world produces. (Long, 142)

The earth is a womb; the seed is also planted in the woman. The rain, like semen, fertilizes. Pyramids are sacred mountains. Gods speak in thunder. Birds are divine messengers. Any number of connections and associations come to mind.

From the very beginning, language undoubtedly has been used to express relationship, to provide a medium for expressing "the shells of all the things that this world produces." Contrary to our atomistic perception, which sees the world in terms of separate, individual objects, some scholars believe that the early stages of language and consciousness were inherently metaphorical, that they represented a holistic view of the world. Sometimes this metaphoric role can be more easily recognized in a foreign language:

> The Eskimo language, being polysynthetic, isn't composed of little words chronologically ordered, but of great, tight conglomerates, like twisted knots, within which concepts are juxtaposed and inseparably fused. Such conglomerates are not "verbs" or "nouns" or even "words"; each is a linguistic expression for an impression forming a unit to the Eskimo. Thus, "the house is red" in Eskimo is phrased "the-house, looking-like-flowing-blood-it-is." (Carpenter, 78)

Martin Buber provides another example:

> We say, "far away"; the Zulu has a sentence word instead that means: "where one cries, 'mother, I am lost.' " (69–70)

English speakers do not experience this interconnectedness directly because the English language evolved in conjunction with the history of Western consciousness and became a fine instrument for reducing reality to its constituent parts, for describing the machinery of the cosmos, for definitions and negotiations in analytic prose. As it grew and evolved, the language slowly became a lumberyard of wooden metaphors, adapting to a highly abstract, atomized world. We are clear that a rose is a rose and not a rock, but we might have difficulties seeing the similarities between flowing blood and running streams, a mountain and a temple, a pregnant woman and a ceramic pot.

We must depend upon figures of speech to provide the necessary analogies for appreciating relationships. *Poetry, art, religion, and mythology are collections of metaphors and symbols necessary for integrating the world.*

Metaphoric Comparison: Subject and Figure

Using language is a complex task because words are a kind of short-hand for reality: the individual letters of words are obviously not the objects designated by them. The word *bird* is not a bird. *Bird* could indicate any number of varieties, shapes, and colors of actual birds. We need to modify *bird* in order to make it meaningful: as in "A small brown sparrow sits in the pine tree." When an even more precise description is important, we can resort to comparison, the root of metaphor, as Howard Nemerov does in the following:

> While I am thinking about metaphor, a flock of purple finches arrives on the lawn. Since I haven't seen these birds for some years, I am only fairly sure of their being in fact purple finches, so I get down Peterson's *Field Guide* and read his description: "Male: About size of House Sparrow, rosy-red, brightest on head and rump." That checks quite well, but his next remark—"a sparrow dipped in raspberry juice"—is decisive: it fits. . . . It is like being told: If you really want to see something, look at something else. (Nemerov, 33)

A fresh and pleasurable comparison is created between the two parts of a metaphor: the *subject*, finches, is compared with the *figure*, a sparrow dipped in raspberry juice.

When we write about nonphysical subjects, such as emotions or attitudes, it is usually necessary to compare them to concrete or physical figures. If we want to describe a marriage that has become habitual and routine, we say, "The marriage has cooled off, the spark is missing." We try to say what it is by saying what it is not, or what it used to be, or what object it reminds us of:

> It is stale as the crumbs
> from a half-remembered
> wedding cake.

A paradox is involved: the more we try to be specific and look closely at something, the more it becomes necessary to deal indirectly with the uniqueness of that thing.

Dead Metaphors and Live Metaphors

After repeated use, some metaphors become dead or wooden: "the legs of a table," "hard as a rock," "the branch bank," "the jet plane went soaring through the air like a bird." Coming across clichés and worn-out metaphors, the reader feels let down, disengaged from the writing.

When a metaphor works well there is a sense of delight, a feeling of satisfaction and rightness about the comparison, based on the similarities and differences between the subject and the figure. How similar is potting to creating a child? If similarities between the subject and figure come to mind too easily, the metaphor approaches a cliché or overworked metaphor. On the other hand, the figure can add a fresh dimension to a common subject like a forest fire:

> The fire ate the forest
> > like a hungry man
> > eating his dinner
> > after a hard day at work.
>
> > > —Barbara B./JH

And how many times have you heard lava compared to pudding?

> Lava bubbling
> like an over-flowing pan
> > of hot thick pudding.
>
> > > —Dean A./JH

The task for the poet is to continually reclaim the essentially metaphorical unity of reality, to re-create connections between the human spirit and the physical world:

> The Negro Speaks of Rivers
>
> I've known rivers:
> I've known rivers ancient as the world and older than the flow
> > of human blood in human veins.
>
> My soul has grown deep like the rivers.
>
> I bathed in the Euphrates when dawns were young.
> I built my hut near the Congo and it lulled me to sleep.
> I looked upon the Nile and raised the pyramids above it.
> I heard the singing of the Mississippi when Abe Lincoln went
> > down to New Orleans, and I've seen its muddy bosom turn
> > all golden in the sunset.

> I've known rivers:
> Ancient, dusky rivers.
> My soul has grown deep like the rivers.
>
> —Langston Hughes

Conventional or Closed Poetry

For many people, poetry means conventional meters and forms, such as sonnets, villanelles, rhymed couplets, quatrains, blank verse, and the like. These forms exist prior to the writing process as literary conventions. They are like empty bottles waiting to be filled by the individual poet.

Rhyme and meter are mnemonic devices. *Mnemonic* comes from the Greek goddess of memory, Mnemosyne, who was also the mother of all the Muses. Before the invention of the printing press, oral poetry was meant to be memorized, recited, and performed. A wandering bard or minstrel might know hundreds of poems; regular sound and rhythm patterns were aids to memory and well suited for musical accompaniment.

Some of the earliest poetry used regular patterns of rhythm and sound. One of the oldest writings in the Bible is the "Song of Moses," celebrating the victory over Pharaoh's army at the Red Sea (c. 12th century B.C.). With this victory song there are "stage directions" for the women's chorus and dancers:

> Miriam, the prophetess, Aaron's sister, took up a timbrel, and all the women followed her with timbrels, dancing. And Miriam led them in the refrain:
> 'Sing of Yahweh: he has covered himself in glory,
> horse and rider he has thrown into the sea.'
>
> (Exodus 15:20–21, *Jerusalem Bible*)

Within this setting it is possible to imagine a ceremony reenacting the victory.

Another example of patterning is the following, in which the Red Sea is referred to as the Sea of Reeds:

> The chariots and the army of Pharaoh he has hurled into the sea;
> the pick of his horsemen lie drowned in the Sea of Reeds.
> The depths have closed over them;
> they have sunk to the bottom like a stone.
> Your right hand, Yahweh, shows majestic in power,
> your right hand, Yahweh, shatters the enemy.
>
> (Exodus 15:4–8)

Although this translation does not break the text visually into couplets, it nevertheless employs a prominent characteristic of Hebrew poetry called "parallelism." The second line of each couplet might repeat the first with a slight variation; or the second line might be antithetical to the first. The first line can be a question and the second an answer. The couplet structure provides an important rhythm for chanting this poetic history, and was probably part of a communal dance pattern.

Traditional poetry follows a basic principle of *repetition* and *variation*: repetition of the beat, the phrase, the line, and then a change which extends the action of the poem and adds variety.

Nursery rhymes are an obvious example of the connection between poetic devices and action:

Ring around the rosy
A pocket full of posies
Ashes, ashes
We all fall down

The repetition of sounds, alliteration and assonance, along with a regular rhythmic pattern of stresses, forms a delightful pattern for circling children who must interrupt their dance by suddenly sitting down. This last act is perfectly parallel to the three stressed syllables of the last three words. Furthermore, a *symbolic* meaning apparently lies hidden behind these innocent lines. The second line probably refers to a cave of flowers in fairyland—a source of fertility and growth; the last line indicates the end of the season and death by the Grim Reaper. A related tradition connects these lines to the black plague of the Middle Ages, in which the "posies" are flowering lesions.

A basic principle is that sound and rhythm should not exist as independent elements, but should support the sense of a poem, as in the following:

Eagle
Its keen eyesight is great.
Its beauty is a wonder.
Its poise in air
Is magnificent thunder.

—Brian H./JH

The danger of closed verse is that it can become mechanical and repetitious. A military cadence is inappropriate for a lullaby. An obvious and discordant separation of form and content occurs in the following excerpt from Longfellow's "A Psalm of Life":

Tell me not, in mournful numbers,
    Life is but an empty dream!—
For the soul is dead that slumbers,
    And things are not what they seem.

Life is real! Life is earnest!
    And the grave is not its goal;
Dust thou art, to dust returnest,
    Was not spoken of the soul.

This stanza form has all the advantages of regularity and repetition—
ease of memorization and music for recitation—but the meter of the
lines marches on irrespective of the ideas and feelings being expressed.

In the following excerpt from Sterling Brown's "Strong Men," repetition and a variety of forms are used to convey Brown's feelings about
the treatment of blacks in this country:

They dragged you from homeland,
They chained you in coffles,
They huddled you spoon-fashion in filthy hatches,
They sold you to give a few gentlemen ease.

They broke you in like oxen,
They scourged you,
They branded you,
They made your women breeders,
They swelled your numbers with bastards . . .
They taught you the religion they disgraced.

You sang:
    Keep a-inchin' along
    Lak a po' inch worm . . .

You sang:
    Bye and bye
    I'm gonna lay down dis heaby load . . .

You sang:
    Walk togedder, chillen,
    Dontcha git weary . . .
        The strong men keep a-comin' on
        The strong men git stronger.

The repeated use of "They" piles up into the large body of anonymous,
oppressive white "Theys" who perpetrated slavery. In contrast are the
shorter excerpts from Negro slave songs and spirituals. The use of dialect
lends authenticity to the songs. The refrain provides a break in the poem
and adds an additional voice, like a choric response. In fact, Brown
makes use of couplet patterns reminiscent of the biblical example at the
beginning of this section. Form is closely wedded to content.

One argument for the use of fixed forms is that they provide a
discipline or challenge for the poet, and are a link to a literary tradi-

tion. There are about three hundred years of English poetry in which the use of preset forms was the norm, and training in scansion was very helpful for both writing and reading poetry.

Teachers and Closed Verse

Many teachers of literature like conventional meters and forms. One attraction of teaching scansion is that meter, rhyme schemes, and stanza patterns are measurable (kind of), and can be tested and graded. So much of poetry seems subjective that anything with the appearance of objectivity is treasured. Exact definitions, labels, and parts are tempting: it might be easier if there were five kinds of novel plots, four kinds of rhyme, three kinds of sonnets, four kinds of metrical feet, five grand subjects, and sixteen minor subjects for poems. But literature, especially modern poetry, has a way of crossing lines and slipping out of definitional boxes.

An educational platitude applied to all parts of the curriculum can be applied here: students must first learn the basics for a given discipline before they are allowed to experiment and explore on their own. Applied to poetry, this means learning conventional English meters and forms, such as the sonnet, before dealing with modern poetry and "free verse." But in reality the English tradition is only one part of the history of poetry. *The real basics begin with language and our need to express who we are and how we are related to this world.*

Open Forms

An alternative idea about rhythm and form is that they can evolve out of the experience being expressed on the page. For each poem the poet creates the form which is uniquely appropriate to the experience or contents of that particular piece.

Prior to the twentieth century, American writers often followed English literary models, especially in poetry. But a real revolution took place in both prose and poetry when writers shifted their models from the written tradition to the spoken. They listened to how flesh-and-blood people spoke, and used that language as a base for dialogue, or the rhythmic unit of an image or metaphor.

One of the first Americans to break with the conventional forms used by British poets was Walt Whitman. He was searching for a kind of poetry consistent with the variety and energy of the American culture. He developed a long, prosy line which is conversational in tone and gives the impression of personal involvement with the subject of the poetry:

> Ah, what can ever be more stately and admirable to me than mast-
> hemm'd Manhattan?
> River and sunset and scallop-edg'd waves of flood-tide?
> The sea-gulls oscillating their bodies, the hay-boat in the twilight,
> and the belated lighter?
> What gods can exceed these that clasp me by the hand, and with
> voices I love call me promptly and loudly by my nighest
> name as I approach?
> What is more subtle than this which ties me to the woman or man
> that looks in my face?
> Which fuses me into you now, and pours my meaning into you?
>
> (from "Crossing Brooklyn Ferry")

Whitman is the father of the long prose line, which has been called "end-stopped free verse." He uses a variety of pauses within his lines, but gives the impression of a continuous monologue. Nevertheless the lines for the most part are unvarying in rhythm and length. Later poets brought more variety to this conversational line by adapting it to changes of emotion and voice.

Americans speak with such freedom; words were quickly borrowed from other languages, and new words were created for factory jobs in Pittsburgh and lumber camps in Minnesota. Subcultures, such as the jazz culture, developed their own vocabulary, and oppressed groups, such as blacks, gave new twists to old words.

The Spoken Word as a Model for Open Forms

Allen Ginsberg wrote poetry in metered verse until he ran across William Carlos Williams and came to realize he was not writing in his own voice:

> Conversations with Williams reinforced the insight, 'cause I went to see him, and he had written down on a piece of paper . . . "I'll kick yuh eye." And he said now you're writing metrical poetry, but how would you measure that funny phrase "I'll kick yuh eye," 'cause it's got a little syncopation in it, "yuh eye," which would be very difficult to describe in a regular meter. What I picked up from him was that he was writing without any rules at all, except listening to rhythm that he heard around him. He was talking rhythms directly from his own voice . . . from the changes that he heard in his own voice or in the Polish workman up and down his block, "I'll kick yuh eye." (142)

We really are such experts at speaking. It is a wonder to observe a young child begin to use language to relate to the world, to make demands, to exclaim, "No! NO! NO!?"—always three or more times.

The challenge for a poet like Lew Welch was how to get the energy of the spoken word onto the written page:

> Once, on the way to Oregon, I stopped at a California winery to get free wine from the tasting room. Just at that time a tour was starting so I decided to go along. A young man of about 23 was the guide and began that strange kind of language guides use, almost a chant: . . . *and on the left a 1500 gallon redwood barrel containing Burgundy kept always at the temperature of*. . . and then he said *Whose kid is that?*
>
> The force of *Whose kid is that* caused everyone to pay attention to the real moment we were all in. A small child was about to fall into a very deep vat of wine.
>
> I vowed, at that moment, that every statement in my poems would have at least the force of *Whose kid is that.*
>
> It is an impossible standard, but a good one. Few really bad lines can stand against it. (5–6)

The spoken voice has accent and pitch, and when we speak we add facial expressions and body gestures. How do these translate to the page?

I tell beginning writing students that poetry is like gossip, animated speech between friends. A poem often begins with an urgent sense of sharing: "Do you know what happened to me last night? In those dark shadows by the back door?" In the 1950s, Anglo poets began to read their poems out loud to audiences; poems were chanted, sung, recited. And an oral tradition with its roots in Native American culture as well as in the ancient bardic tradition of Europe spread across the country, continuing to the present day.

Rhythm and Organic Forms

The most personal sense of rhythm comes from our own bodies: the pumping heart, the feel of one's pulse, the monthly menstrual cycle, the ups and downs of moods and feelings. Rhythm is involved in passing through the different stages of life: from birth to maturity to death. Nature is full of sounds and rhythms: wind, water, trees, storm. Nature is filled with forms: the cycle of day and night, the turn of the seasons, the large patterns of earth and sky. Species and their relationships have forms—that is a simple fact. Translating these forms into poetry, however, is more complicated.

The secret of reading metered poetry is discovering the pattern of stresses and relating this pattern to the poem's meaning. Stress is important in open forms as well, but, in addition, the sounds and shapes of the lines in open forms can visually indicate meaning. Imagine a game of charades in which someone molds her whole body into the topic or theme: the easier ones are simple figures, like a tree or a chair. In poetry this corresponds to the concrete poem:

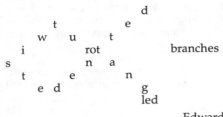

—Edward P./C

The charade player can become a thin, falling shape for rain and a bright, shining face for a sunflower, but more complex physical and emotional experiences are difficult to express. How does she become a thick, deliberate shape for arguments with her husband or an irregular, hesitant shape for her fears of an empty parking lot at night? Even in charades these shapes are not always self-evident or clear, but that is the basic idea for open poetic forms.

Uptight, fearful situations demand uptight sounds, like *pinch, twist, gasp,* and *shudder.* Soft moments where the living is easy need solemn, smooth sounds, like *shadows, mood, tranquil, mellow, yellow.* Exciting moments could use quick and light sounds: *pep, titter, pop, flight.* Strong and decisive actions use strong rhythms and forceful sounds: *kick, throttle, embrace, break, conquer.* And on and on.

What are the sounds and rhythms of a modern city? Horns, buses, brakes slamming, sirens wailing, hammers, tires. To express this mood, we can use onomatopoetic words: *hum, crack, blast, moan, roar, crunch, buzz.*

Omitting end rhyme does not mean there is no rhyme at all; poems are full of sounds that sound alike, or almost sound alike.

The careful use of line lengths and stresses in the following poem suggests the poet's feelings:

> Waking to the morning smell of
> Bacon
> Coffee
> Ham and eggs. The comfort of the cozy kitchen
>
> My father smelling of aftershave
> His masculine aroma of strength & protection

He's gone now
We no longer share breakfast in the morning
Mom and I don't eat
My brother gulps cereal
I start the day by myself

—Jennifer E./HS

The stressed words *bacon, coffee,* and *ham and eggs* suggest the building blocks of the family security, along with the presence of the father. A kind of disintegration is marked in the last stanza: four out of the five lines are stressed on the first syllables, and four out of five are brief, abrupt statements, pointing to the bleak sadness brought about by the father's departure.

Using the resources of language to capture various situations becomes a challenge. With open forms there is no way of knowing prior to the creative process what the poem might look like—or sound like. For the writer, the form must be flexible enough to support whatever is being expressed through it; after all, form can be like a tourniquet on an otherwise healthy limb. For the reader, it is a question of appropriateness, and the integration of the poem's parts.

When the various tools of sound, rhythm, and form are intertwined with an honest poetic voice, a strong poem may result. In this final poem the repetition, the stresses, and the shape of the indentations suggest a piling up of depressing symptoms, reinforcing the clarity and honesty of the emotions:

You know the feeling you get
When you haven't eaten
    And your head aches—
        And limbs shake—
            And you want to cry—
I hate that!

You know the feeling you get
When you eat too much
    And your back hurts—
        And your stomach throbs—
            And your clothes bind—
                And you want to throw up—
I hate that!

You know the feeling you get
When you take a shot
    And the alcohol's cold—
        And the needle's sharp—
            And it hurts going in—
                And it hurts coming out—
I hate that!

You know the feeling you get
When you have diabetes
And everyday it's the same—
And you shake—
And you're weak—
And you're not quite normal—
I hate that!

—Michele L./C

Writing Suggestions for Classroom Use

1. After discussing what makes an image vivid or vital, pair off with another student and write each other's portrait.

2. Describe in writing an object, person, or feeling without naming the item directly: a favorite food, a fruit or vegetable, a body part, a person across the room, a moment of fear or sadness, the feelings attending the birth of a child.

3. Expand or deepen the following images with adjectives and other modifiers: her or his lips, a ripe melon, a dark pool of water, my face in the mirror, Grandmother's kitchen, falling in love for the first time.

4. Use metaphors or similes to answer these questions:
   How is a dragonfly like a helicopter?
   How is a ball like an echo?
   Which is faster, a whisper or a shout?
   How is falling in love like parachuting from a plane?

5. Use metaphors or similes to describe the following: a sunset, two seals playing, the best pizza in town, the biggest football player, the fastest male and female runners, your girlfriend's (boyfriend's) smile, the latest rock band (dance, fast food, style of dress), your favorite teacher (friend, parent, sport, movie star), the craziest haircut, the ugliest car (school building, sunset, street, city).

6. A concrete poem visually resembles its subject; write one.

7. Sit quietly. List all of the sounds and rhythms in your current world. How might you communicate these sounds and rhythms in writing?

References

Boswell, James. 1953. *The Life of Samuel Johnson*. Edited by R. W. Chapman. Oxford, England: Oxford University Press.

Brown, Sterling. 1972. "Strong Men." In *Modern and Contemporary Afro-American Poetry*, edited by Bernard W. Bell. Boston: Allyn and Bacon, Inc.

Buber, Martin. 1970. *I and Thou*. New York: Charles Scribner's Sons.

Carpenter, Edmund. 1973. *Eskimo Realities*. New York: Holt, Rinehart and Winston.

Fussell, Paul. 1979. *Poetic Meter and Poetic Form*. Rev. ed. New York: Random House.

Ginsberg, Allen. 1974. *Allen Verbatim: Lectures on Poetry, Politics, Consciousness*, edited by Gordon Ball. New York: McGraw-Hill Book Company.

Hughes, Langston, and Arna Bontemps. 1949. *The Poetry of the Negro: 1746–1949*. Garden City, N.Y.: Doubleday & Co.

Jones, Alexander, ed. 1966. *Jerusalem Bible*. Garden City, N.Y.: Doubleday & Co.

Long, Charles H. 1963. *Alpha: The Myths of Creation*. New York: George Braziller.

Longfellow, Henry Wadsworth. 1974. "A Psalm of Life." In *The American Tradition in Literature*, edited by Sculley Bradley, et al. 4th ed. New York: Grosset & Dunlap.

Nemerov, Howard. 1972. *Reflexions on Poetry & Poetics*. New Brunswick, N.J.: Rutgers University Press.

Pope, Alexander. 1959. "Essay on Criticism." In *Major British Writers*, edited by G. B. Harrison. Vol. 1. New York: Harcourt, Brace & World.

Pound, Ezra. 1972. "Vorticism (1914)." In *Modern Literary Criticism 1900–1970*, edited by Lawrence I. Lipking and A. Walton Litz. New York: Atheneum.

Thrall, W. F., Addison Hibbard, and C. Hugh Holman. 1960. *A Handbook to Literature*. 2nd ed. New York: The Odyssey Press.

Toelken, Barre. 1969. "Pretty Language of Yellowman." *Genre* 2, no. 3: 231.

Turco, Lewis. 1986. *The New Book of Forms: A Handbook of Poetics*. Hanover and London: University Press of New England.

Welch, Lew. 1973. *Ring of Bone: Collected Poems 1950–1971*. Edited by Donald Allen. Bolinas, Calif.: Grey Fox Press.

Whitman, Walt. 1973. *Leaves of Grass*. Edited by Sculley Bradley and Harold W. Blodgett. New York: W. W. Norton & Co.

3 Bugaboos and Red Herring: Misconceptions about Poetry

A number of misconceptions about poetry continue to clutter the path for writer, reader, and teacher. After a brief discussion of each of the bugaboos, I provide a reasonable alternative.

1. Poetry is high culture.

Culture, like *virtue*, is one of those highly malleable words, suitable for various occasions and perspectives. Culture is often associated with the refinement of mind, emotions, manners, and taste through the cultivation of ideas and the arts. This kind of culture is linked to the rise of civilization: it makes cultivated, "well rounded" humans out of potential barbarians. On the surface these seem like good intentions. Problems arise, however, when a distinction is made between "high culture"— such as great books and opera—and "low or mass culture"—such as the folk songs and dances of a particular ethnic group or region.

Growing up in a small Midwestern town just after World War II, I learned in school that "real culture" resided in cities, especially East Coast cities, and was something like the Metropolitan Opera, which visited our region once a year, was expensive, and was very foreign to our lives. In contrast, George Larson, who lived just a block away, played the fiddle and accordian by ear. He knew hundreds of songs, both American and old country; his music wasn't "real" culture.

Behind the distinction between high and low culture resides the ugly beast of class distinctions: a way to distinguish one group from another and a way to sell or "market" the arts. Too often, high culture has meant Western, European, white American, male culture, where the value is measured by the price tag.

Poetry as high culture is for the discriminating reader; it is taught like a mysterious brand of medicine. Although you might not like it or understand it, or find it relevant, IT IS GOOD FOR YOU.

Alternative: Poetry is democratic.

I prefer the idea that poetry arises out of the broad spectrum of human activity—from the incantations of medicine men to the fantasies

44

of debutantes—and is addressed to all segments of the human community:

> No word meaning "art" occurs in Eskimo, nor does "artist"; there are only people. Nor is any distinction made between utilitarian and decorative objects. The Eskimo simply say, "A man should do all things properly." (Carpenter, 8)

(And a woman also, I assume.)

2. Poetry consists of elevated ideas in elevated language.

The notion of special poetic themes expressed in a special poetic language is related to misconception #1: poetry as high culture includes themes such as the beauty of nature, the elusiveness of true love, and the nobility of a king, as well as a dignified language of figures and meters. This assumption about poetry is a matter of social and historical convention: what topics are permissible in polite society or in mixed company, which topics are taboo, which ideas are in and which are out.

For centuries in Western society there was a clear line between what was publicly acceptable and what was privately fantasized, felt, and said. Can you *imagine* the shock in the late eighteenth century when Jean Jacques Rousseau crossed this line? Here are the first words of his *Confessions*:

> I am commencing an undertaking, hitherto without precedent, and which will never find an imitator. I desire to set before my fellows the likeness of a man in all the truth of nature, and that man myself.
>
> Myself alone! I know the feelings of my heart, and I know men. I am not made like any of those I have seen; I venture to believe that I am not made like any of those who are in existence. If I am not better, at least I am different. Whether Nature has acted rightly or wrongly in destroying the mould in which she cast me, can only be decided after I have been read.
>
> Let the trumpet of the Day of Judgment sound when it will, I will present myself before the Sovereign Judge with this book in my hand. I will say boldly: "This is what I have done, what I have thought, what I was. I have told the good and the bad with equal frankness." (3)

And so he did, thus creating a revolution in Western letters and consciousness. Ever since, in one form or another, poets and writers have been preparing their books, their confessions, to present to the Sovereign Judge, searching for the full likeness of what it means to be human.

Alternative: Poetry embraces the entire spectrum of heart and mind, and the total resources of language.

Prior to the actual writing of the poem, no deed or word can be declared unfit for poetry, "unpoetic." The poem might be disagreeable—even offensive—and we might choose not to read it, but as long as it was written by a person rather than a machine it can be called poetry. Poets in prison and Vietnam vets, for example, have enlarged our consciousness with the truth of their experiences.

3. Great poetry contains universal meanings.

Shakespeare is often used as the standard of universality; despite the fact that he wrote over three hundred years ago, the great themes developed in his plays transcend the particulars of the Elizabethan era and continue to involve and challenge us today. I. A. Richards, for his part, provided five themes which inspire sincere feelings:

  i. Man's loneliness (the isolation of the human situation).
 ii. The facts of birth, and of death, in their inexplicable oddity.
iii. The inconceivable immensity of the Universe.
 iv. Man's place in the perspective of time.
  v. The enormity of his ignorance. (273)

   We could easily add to this list: the inevitable conflict between parents and children, the use of war and aggression to settle conflicts, the dominance of men over women, and so on. The preacher in Ecclesiastes says, "There is nothing new under the sun," and when it comes to human nature, that is certainly true.

   The young writer, however, needs to be reminded that the art of Shakespeare and Whitman and Faulkner had its roots in the particular, in people and places. Some teachers confuse universality with generality, and thereby lead students to believe that their writing should be sufficiently general to appeal to a wide audience. What happens then is that students write poems filled with platitudes about the human condition and the vastness of the cosmos.

Alternative: A young writer should deal with the realities of his or her own experience, and the universals will take care of themselves.

The challenge for the young poet is to probe the particulars of his or her own personal experience in order to discover what is unique and vital to his or her existence. We hope that in this process the young writer will discover relationships and that tangled web of hopes and fears, successes and failures which is common to humanity.

Therein resides the paradox: when a poet is specific and concrete, the reader's imagination is engaged and the experience of the poem can be shared (sharing suggests some aspect of universality); but when the poet drifts into generalities and abstractions, the reader also drifts into this mist of vagaries and is forced to invent an airplane of his or her own design.

4. Poetry is essentially a puzzle.

Because of poetic devices such as symbol, metaphor, irony, and paradox, and because most poets in anthologies lived in earlier and different times and places, the "meaning" of a poem can be hidden below the surface—often, with great poems, WAY BELOW THE SURFACE. According to this view, the reader's task is to excavate and decipher the layers of meanings until the poem can be rendered in an acceptable paraphrase.

Students are occasionally led to believe that there is only *one correct paraphrase*, a single meaning which the teacher guards like a golden treasure and shares with only the most worthy students.

Some poems can be paraphrased, some cannot; given the ambiguous nature of language, all poems—of whatever length—have multiple meanings. But the real point is that a poem is more than prose meaning cloaked in poetic ornament. A poem is an experience, not simply a puzzle to be solved.

Alternative: The first task for a reader is to get inside the poetic experience, whether it is mental, emotional, visceral, or all three.

Like Emily Dickinson in the "Introduction," above, A. E. Housman maintains that poetry is more physical than intellectual, and is best recognized by the symptoms it produces:

> One of these symptoms was described in connection with another object by Eliphaz the Temanite: "A spirit passed before my face: the hair of my flesh stood up." Experience has taught me, when I am shaving of a morning, to keep watch over my thoughts, because, if a line of poetry strays into my memory, my skin bristles so that the razor ceases to act . . . accompanied by a shiver down the spine; there is another which consists in a constriction of the throat and a precipitation of water to the eyes; and there is a third which I can only describe by borrowing a phrase from one of Keats' last letters, where he says, speaking of Fanny Brawne, "everything that reminds me of her goes through me like a spear." The seat of this sensation is the pit of the stomach. (46)

Would it make sense to test poetry students by attaching electrodes to various parts of their bodies and registering their physiological responses to poems? Excitement, rather than puzzlement, is appropriate to reading poetry. One way to measure this excitement is by the creativity which follows it.

5. Real poetry uses conventional meters and rhymes.

This issue was discussed in chapter 2, but it deserves some review. Behind this kind of definition is a whole concern with pigeonholing and labeling: the need to put experience into boxes, to distinguish one literary genre from another, to separate one literary form from another, to uphold a literary tradition, to defend the idea of "classics."

Probably this bugaboo should be listed as number one above; a majority of students seem to carry the idea out of high school that poetry means meter and rhyme. Ironically, most of them have not been led to make the connection between poetry and the lyrics which fill their ears.

How do we cut through all the wrappings and attend in a fresh and immediate way to our own flesh and blood? How do we learn to sing and tell our stories in a society of increasing anonymity?

There is one overall issue behind poetry, behind all creativity: whether we feel at home in the world, whether we love and care for it, whether we reach across racial, religious, and ethnic lines to brotherhood and sisterhood; or whether we feel alienated and estranged from the world and its peoples, and thereby treat them with anger and exploitation.

Alternative: Real poetry uses the full resources of the human heart, of language, sound, and rhythm, to create a human habitation for our sojourn on earth.

References

Carpenter, Edmund. 1973. *Eskimo Realities.* New York: Holt, Rinehart and Winston.

Housman, A. E. 1944. *The Name and Nature of Poetry.* New York: Macmillan.

Richards, I. A. 1929. *Practical Criticism.* New York: Harcourt, Brace and World, Inc.

Rousseau, Jean Jacques. n.d. [1788]. *The Confessions of Jean Jacques Rousseau.* New York: Random House.

4 Writing Poems: Some Suggestions

The one rule for writing poetry is that there are no absolute rules for poetry, or for any of the arts. Based on my experiences and the advice of other writers, I can make suggestions about what seems to have worked in the past, but each individual must find his or her own way to the blank page, using whatever is helpful in this book and disregarding the rest.

There are two sides to writing poetry: craft and consciousness. Craft involves learning the resources of language, its limits, and its possibilities. Consciousness involves learning how to see and use the inner world and the outer world.

A person may be a talented writer but have very little to say; or a person might have unique perceptions about him- or herself and the world but lack the language tools to express them. Both sides need practice and study.

First, however, a commitment to language is necessary: choosing to see the world in terms of words. This means spending time with words, continually translating experiences into words, playing with words, probing against the barriers of language, taking delight in puns and conceits, reading books and more books, and carrying a notebook around with you.

Language is all around us. Daily we are bombarded with media language and consumer language and the latest fad language. It is a real question whether an individual can use language honestly, to say something real from the heart without lapsing into cant or jargon.

Creative writing is a process of cutting through everyday, dead uses of language to some fresh expression which brings vitality and perspective to an otherwise inert and irrelevant slice of reality.

What seems like language play can end up in a poem:

What Is Real Loneliness

—I wonder

I know 3 A.M. loneliness is lonelier
    than 11 P.M. loneliness

49

11 promises sleep
3 doesn't
11 promises noise
3 doesn't
11 promises you you're not too far gone
3 doesn't
Real loneliness must be when
11 promises you 3.
                                        —Keith N./C

Writing Tools

William Faulkner was once asked what would be the best environment
for a writer, and he replied,

> The only environment the artist needs is whatever peace, whatever
> solitude, and whatever pleasure he can get at not too high a
> cost. . . . My own experience has been that the tools I need for my
> trade are paper, tobacco, food and a little whiskey. (69)

What else is helpful to the writer?

A good dictionary and thesaurus
Paper and pencil
Time

I once taught a course with a writer who recommended cutting your
own quills and making your own ink. And he was adamant about
writing the first draft by hand. I cannot testify to quills and homemade
ink, but I prefer writing the first draft by hand. I like the impression
given by pencil: it is temporary and experimental, easily erased or
scratched out. Later drafts may be typed, but typing the first draft makes
it seem finished and permanent, resistant to change.

Already I hear the protests: typing is so much faster, I need to keep
up with my thoughts, typing is neater. My reply is that advantages arise
from going in the opposite direction, by slowing down your consciousness to the speed of your hand. A slower speed allows for detours
and free association, unforeseen digressions and happy accidents—a
stroll through the forest, as opposed to barreling down the interstate
highway. What's the hurry? You'll miss all the scenery.

Writing Regularly and Journals

Little needs to be said about writing regularly. Writing is like any other
skill: it needs to be practiced. I believe it is better to write a little bit

every day than to write larger amounts once a week. Writing takes a kind of attentiveness, an alertness, a receptivity; and these are best practiced often. Furthermore, it takes time to loosen the material within, which can be viscous and thick. And just as important, it takes diligence to work through the clichés floating around in one's consciousness, the easy phrases, those words that habitually come to mind first.

A journal has two basic functions. As a *diary*, it is a place to record personal experiences, from the mundane to the exotic, a regular taking of one's pulse: thoughts, attitudes, dreams, diet, whatever. Or the question: "How am I doing today?" As a *vehicle for experimentation and discovery*, a journal is a safe place to play with language and one's consciousness: here in privacy the writer can record secret thoughts and fantasies, test taboos, explore intimacy, and experiment with words. I record bits of overheard conversation, ideas for poems, books to read, bizarre twists of mind, new perceptions. Because of this exploratory function, some psychologists use journals in therapy.

It sometimes happens that while I am recording a rather ordinary daily event, a door will open within and material will burst (or float) into consciousness: some bit of history, materials from childhood, a former friend, a distant city. A feeling of warmth or energy will accompany this buried material, as if it were being released for my enjoyment and use. And, for a time, I can follow through with this revelation on paper, one image leading to another.

The process of claiming the contents of one's own psyche is what I mean by *discovery*. Something is revealed in the very act of writing, something that otherwise would have remained hidden. A connection is made. And a line of verse, even a whole poem, might emerge.

Keep a notebook or journal handy while reading: the whole associative process can result from exposing yourself to someone else's poem, novel, or journal entry.

Organizing the Journal

A journal provides a storehouse of material for later use: for entertainment, for poems, for therapy. But one must be able to retrieve material to use it.

First, use a hardbound notebook. Spiral-bound softcover notebooks inevitably break apart and are lost. A journal should also be the right size to be portable, like a mouse hiding in your pocket. Choose the size that seems right to you.

Next, use some kind of organizational method for separating various kinds of writing and information. I make a simple distinction: the right-hand pages are for diary entries—places visited on a trip, foods eaten, things said and done. The left-hand pages are for special observations, fancy images, lines of poetry, remembrances of things past. I usually begin writing on the right side, but switch to the left whenever the writing, however humbly, begins to lift itself above the prosaic and ordinary.

Two Paths of Creativity

Creativity can be divided into two different activities: *manipulation* and *letting go.*

Manipulation involves the conscious arrangement or ordering of materials to produce a final product: the process of *making* something. It consists of organizing materials according to a preconceived plan—a structuring from beginning to end—and is appropriate for constructing a house or writing an essay.

For the young poet, creating by manipulation usually means having an idea or experience suitable for a poem and then fitting words to it, translating the experience from the mind to the page. Often the young writer measures success by whether the written translation corresponds to the original mental image.

To a certain extent, all writing involves some manipulation; writing fiction, for example, can mean plot outlines, strategies for characterization, models for dialogue, and techniques for establishing a setting.

Manipulation, however, can be a straitjacket for writing poetry, a kind of closure for the consciousness. Too much control can lead to a mechanical poem, a poem that is well constructed, but also wooden and dull.

Creating by letting go, in contrast, is especially suited for any writing that is exploratory, that seeks new associations and connections. It means beginning the process of writing without preconceived ideas about the direction and end of the process. It means being as open as possible to the flow of one's consciousness from image to image, pattern to pattern. It takes a kind of faith not to control or force the material but to *let go,* to discover in the process of writing itself what it is you are writing about. A. E. Housman uses an unusual metaphor for this process:

> I think that the production of poetry, in its first stage, is less an active than a passive and involuntary process; and if I were obliged not to define poetry, but to name the class of things to which it belongs, I should call it a secretion; whether a natural secretion, like turpentine in the fir, or a morbid secretion, like the pearl in the oyster. (47–48)

The images might be more forthcoming than secretion or oozing—for example, an eruption or a shower—but the idea is to allow for the unconscious to participate in the creative process, to allow the being within to emerge.

If creating by manipulation could be likened to the construction of an edifice, then creating by letting go is more akin to giving birth. It is not any easier to describe this process than it is to illuminate the daydream or the reverie—to which it is akin. A. A. Milne captures the spirit of letting go with Winnie the Pooh:

> What shall we do about poor little Tigger?
> If he never eats nothing he'll never get bigger.
> He doesn't like honey and haycorns and thistles
> Because of the taste and because of the bristles.
> And all the good things which an animal likes
> Have the wrong sort of swallow or too many spikes.

"He's quite big enough anyhow," said Piglet.
"He isn't really very big."
"Well, he seems so."
Pooh was thoughtful when he heard this, and then he murmured to himself:

> But whatever his weight in pounds, shillings and ounces,
> He always seems bigger because of his bounces.

"And that's the whole poem," he said. "Do you like it, Piglet?"
"All except the shillings," said Piglet. "I don't think they ought to be there."
"They wanted to come in after the pounds," explained Pooh, "so I let them. It is the best way to write poetry, letting things come."
"Oh, I didn't know," said Piglet.

(*The House at Pooh Corner*, 30–31)

Automatic Writing/Free Flow Writing

Letting go is not as easy as it sounds. With the first appearance of a blank sheet of paper, one is tempted to think and to plot a series of words across the page, to construct meaningful sentences, to make sense.

Another difficulty with letting go is the censor in the head, the one that looks over your shoulder as you write. Because of conditioning, because of embarrassment or fear, it takes practice to be honest on the page, to open up—even in private.

The journal is a good place to begin with what has been called "automatic writing," "free flow writing," or "writing without focus." Here is one way of proceeding:

> Sit quietly, relax. Allow anything to drift into your consciousness. Write it down, and continue to write without any preconceived direction or purpose. Let yourself wander to any subject. Write quickly. Do not stop to make complete sentences, to make sense or be coherent. Continue for at least ten minutes.

This is a good way to begin any writing session; it is like the stretching exercises a jogger does. Sometimes usable material results from this process, and sometimes it is simply a way of loosening up.

The idea of letting go is an important reminder that the creative process is as much a matter of allowing something to happen as it is of making something happen:

> Ready to Begin
>
> Clearing away the normal
> patterns and wastes of my day,
> I prepare to see what is there,
> to know, through the words,
> what was waiting for me.
> Clearing the path
> for the end to start,
> one waits for what is
> as one waits on creation.
>
> —V. B. Price

What Do I Write About?

Part II of *Word Weaving* is about all the things there are to write about. For now, there is only one place to begin writing, and in my case that is with *me*, and in your case, with *you*:

> If you could document—I don't mean "document" because it's not altogether documentary, of course—but if you could document the imagination, experiences, everything, even some wit, whatever, of one life, one life, however long it may last, it might be of some value to someone someday just to say, well, this human being lived from 1928 to whenever, and this is what she had to say about her life. And that's really all I know. I don't know anything more cosmic, anyway. (Anne Sexton, 310)

Young poets are sometimes told that they must find their own voices, that a poet must dig around inside until he or she finds a single, mellifluous voice waiting to sing. But inside is a multitude of voices, a whole chorus straining for the microphone:

> Few of us know the fantastic characters, emotions, perceptions, and demons that inhabit the theaters that are our minds. We are

encouraged to tell a single (true) story, construct a consistent character, fix an identity. We are thus defined more by neglected possibilities than by realized ones. We rehearse and repeat a monotonous monologue while heroes and villains, saints and madmen, ascetics and libertines wait in the wings for a chance to seize center stage and run wild. . . . Every I is a we. We can become authentically public only by first going to the depths of the private. (Keen and Fox, 9–10)

All those bits and pieces inside me, and I once thought I should try to make sense of them, integrate them into a coherent persona. But no, the real task is to give them expression: to take all the fragments of one's life—past histories, ancestors, children—and make a crazy quilt out of them. Not in one poem or story, but patch by patch, section by section—out of the rags of one's experience.

When a student exclaims, "I have a great idea for a poem, but I don't know where to begin!" I often say, "Begin with your body! Always begin with your body." The mind so easily deceives us; it tricks us into thinking that our ideas are original, that we can actually think for ourselves. But there is no fooling the body. It can be covered by cosmetics and doused with deodorants and perfumes, but it is our testament to mortality, it is the most intimate piece of parchment recording the vicissitudes of time. Every five years, a writer should stand naked in front of a full-length mirror and then write the next installment of "An Ode to My Body."

"Drama" is a handy metaphor for what we write about: all the dramas of our lives—the small, everyday dramas, as well as the large, climactic ones. The crises and victories, the twists and turns, the discoveries under rocks, the light bulb flashing on and off upstairs. The setting of poetry is Shakespeare's "All the world's a stage"; on a smaller scale it is also the gossip we share over the back fence.

Most dramas have a climax: a twist or turn where a new perception is introduced. In a poem, this is the moment of surprise or discovery, the place where the poem turns, where something tickles our spines, or taps our shoulders from behind, or reaches some resolution.

The Rough Draft

Here are some guidelines for writing the first rough draft:

Do not try to rhyme.

Do not worry about line length or form.

Do not worry about spelling or making complete sentences.

Do not be concerned about where the poem is going, whether it makes sense, where it might end.

Do not be concerned about being understood by potential readers or the internal censor.

The task is to remain as open and "irresponsible" as possible, avoiding closure by extraneous concerns which interrupt the flow of words.

Warm-Up Exercises

The object of the following exercises is simply to get students writing, to stimulate their imagination and enable them to generate raw material for poems.

1. *Repeatable phrases* may include the following:
   "If I were a _____, I would _____."
   "I'd rather be a _____ than a _____."
   "Once I was a _____, now I'm a _____."
   "Yesterday..., today...."

   > I'd rather be a shark than a shrimp.
   > Once I was an idea, now I am a book.
   > Once I was a whale, now I am a can of oil.
   >
   > Yesterday you could hear my cat's sharp meows
   >   Today she is too worn-out to purr.
   > Yesterday her world was bright orange
   >   Today it is dark blue.
   >   —Edward R./JH

2. *Repeatable stems* and *initiating phrases* provide other starting points for the imagination:
   "Winter is ..."   "Spring is ..."
   "Love is ..."   "Hate is ..."
   "Cool is ..."   "Hot is ..."

   > Cool is the way hair shines in the sun.
   > Cool is moving to the mountains.
   >   —JH students

   "I remember ..."
   "I dream of ..."
   "I used to believe ..."
   "This morning I woke up ..."

This morning I woke up in the
city dump. I was an old play doll. All my
clothes were torn and my shoes were
torn. And magic markers were written on my
face. I was thrown by a little girl who
didn't like me any more.

—Chary C./JH

3. *Making lists* is another excellent way of generating material. For example, write down the following:

   five things you'd take to a desert island (or to Mars)

   three important people (animals, birds) in your life

   three things you do on mountains (at a lake or the ocean)

   the stuff in your closet

4. *Using the secondary senses*: I bring to class a bag of small objects, such as erasers, coins, tacks, paper clips, and buttons. I have students close their eyes, pull out an object, and discover its qualities with senses other than their sight. Then I ask them to write a poem in which they use their perceptions of the objects to make comparisons with people or situations.

5. *Miscellaneous stimuli*: I have found that many other simple stimuli can promote writing, including music, pictures, and 3 × 5 cards with phrases on them.

6. *Synesthetic exercises* can stretch the imagination:

   What is thinner, day or night?
   What is heavier, red or green?
   What is lighter, a song or silence?
   (suggested by Stephanie Levy)

Showing versus Telling

As a general rule, it is preferable for the young writer to show the reader his or her experience rather than talk *about* the experience. When dealing with personal materials in a poem, it is tempting to explain the meanings and importance of the experience, rather than simply present the experience on the page and leave the interpretation to the reader. Whenever we explain ourselves to the reader, we step back from the experience in order to make observations about it, and in doing so we distance the reader from the work.

The writer is an insider with experiences, inviting the reader to an inside view. I am fairly certain that I have very little to tell others *about* life and its ultimate meanings, but I have a great deal to share about my *experiences,* my life's story.

Even though I do not have specific goals for each poem, I have a general goal: to get closer to my experience and discover the nooks and crannies that lie hidden within it. I want to participate as fully as possible in my life, and not simply be an observer of its passing.

Large numbers of people in this country are spectators: they watch others talk, watch others play music, watch football, watch basketball, watch sitcoms. It seems like there are more and more administrators watching over fewer and fewer doers. I am concerned about the passivity built into electronics, and the endless number of jobs involved with paper pushing and paper sorting—links in a chain.

Some poets are like nineteenth-century landscape painters: observing life from the outside, painting, in essence, "still lifes," with everything stillborn, frozen, and tranquil. In a writing workshop I taught in the early 1970s, a young woman observed that the men and the women in the class wrote very differently. The men wrote about action events, with things happening in their poems: driving cars, making love, hiking in the mountains, and so forth. The women wrote about experiences from a distance, passively, as if they were reflecting about them, weighing and judging them. "How come?" I asked. The women explained that it was partly the result of stereotyping and early conditioning: men could be active, could sow their wild oats, but women were supposed to be the arbiters of values and morality, the preservers of culture and decency. Thus they were taught to distance themselves and to evaluate events. Fortunately, society is changing.

Concrete Language versus Abstract Language

Concrete language is the language of the senses: what we see, hear, taste, smell, touch. When we write, we need to use our own concrete language rather than some "artificial" poetic language. Leave abstractions to the philosophers, theologians, and politicians. If Charlie built his first bubble car on Elm Street in Scrub-Brush, Wyoming, these particulars help to locate the poem. I prefer a poem that is located in a particular time or place or both to one that is floating free through a mist of abstractions.

Closely related to the dangers of abstraction are cosmic topics described with cosmic words. Some topics are so vast they invite vagueness and the void itself: existence, eternity, the universe, infinity, the immensity of space, eons of time, cosmic enlightenment, everlasting love.

Other themes have been treated so often it is difficult to write something fresh and exciting about them: love in the springtime, the joys of friendship, the miraculous power of God, the drunks on skid row, the happiness of marriage, the ignorance of the president, last night's sunset.

And some words or phrases are so broad that they must be roped and tied down to a particular situation in order to be used successfully: *peace, truth, love, wisdom, salvation, alienation, racism, sexism, war, religion, being an American*, and so on.

The Basic Forms

One way to think about form is in terms of function: how the poem is used in the world, how we interact with the drama around us.

1. *Song, lyric*: We sing and celebrate, shout our joys and cry out sorrows—songs of love and union, songs of sadness and solitude. Often we also feel like dancing.

2. *Hymn, chant*: A hymn is a particular kind of song, with its roots in the religious festival. Traditionally it is directed at a god or goddess, is sacred in nature, and is used for praise, thanksgiving, or supplication. A chant uses simple, limited melodies with repetition, usually for liturgical purposes.

3. *Stream of consciousness, dream, and reverie*: By paying attention to the shape and movement of consciousness—as in a daydream or reverie—this kind of poem allows us to share our inner lives. It is the poem of meditation or contemplation. This poem moves by imagistic association rather than by logic or common sense. (Gaston Bachelard provides a full explanation of this kind of writing in *The Poetics of Reverie*.)

4. *Story, narration*: Poems may be written to share personal and family stories: the long journey to this place, the struggles to keep the present from falling into chaos, the desire to die with dignity—to name a few of the stories.

5. *Physical shape*: Another way to handle form is through the visual shape of the poem: fat poems, skinny poems, poems that fall down the page, antiphonal poems (two voices answering each other, e.g., work gangs on the railroad, families at mealtime), proverbs or sayings, concrete poems. The following poem uses this technique.

```
That
      buff           like
            a        hair  my
            lo    has          mother
                               in
                           the
                               morning
```
                           —Eddie M./JH

5. *Miscellaneous forms*: These may include menu poems, letter poems,
   advertisement poems, photograph poems, TV script poems, holiday poems, protest poems, major/minor event poems . . . the list goes
   on and on.

For dozens of other forms, see Lewis Turco's *The New Book of Forms:
A Handbook of Poetics.*

Some beginning poets tend to write one-picture poems, like a single
scene or happening, a single slice of an emotion, a burst of song, one
tantalizing dish from the banquet. With confidence and experience, the
impetus is to include more and more material in the poem, to sustain
the lines and stanzas until everyone and everything are included. In
other words, there is the urge to write longer poems made up of several
parts—an entire album rather than a single snapshot. It takes a kind
of faith to move from one scene to the next, from the present to the
past, from inside to outside and back—a moving collage. The following poem moves easily through time—past, present, and future—and
communicates not just one picture but many.

Uncle Billy

Uncle Billy,
where did you go?
Did you leave because you wanted to?
Didn't you want to see me grow
to laugh in the sun?
To fish with you?
Chase butterflies off your wheelchair?

Why did you leave me so soon?
You never finished making my model airplane
or my rose placemat.
You did give me
the Christmas character in the yard.
Mickey, Pluto, and even Santa.
The races you let me win
on my tricycle.

Uncle Billy
why did you leave me so soon?

There were still so many kites to be flown
from your lap.
So many games with Taffy dog,
and rides in your wheelchair.

When I see you again,
will you be busy running, hunting
and hiking?
How about water-skiing?
Maybe just you and me
feeling that ice cold water of the creek
on our toes.

—Kris W./HS

Line Lengths and Stanzas

At least initially, the sense of the poem and its rhythm can serve as
an aid to structure: a line ends when there is a pause, whether that
occurs after one word in the line or ten. Each line must carry the poem
along, so it is rare that the words *a* or *the* will constitute a whole line,
but it's possible.

Stanzas are the larger units of the unfolding poem, often held together
by a theme or pattern of images. During the process of revision, the
sections of a poem often become clearer: places of stress and pause
or places of voice change, where the poem goes on a detour.

Revising and Critiquing

First, some thought should be given to the reasons for revising any piece
of writing. A poem by a beginning writer might express exactly what
this writer intended; but—a large BUT—does the poem communicate
this experience to the reader? If not, why not? I might ask the writer
to talk about his or her piece of writing, and if the verbal description
is more animated and vivid than the original, written version, I say,
"Write that!"

Who can account for what happens when we actually sit down to
write, often in a state of excitement? We get involved with introductions, explanations, detours, apologies, pretensions, circumlocutions,
and deadwood. Revision is the process of discovering the actual poem
within the raw material of the first draft or drafts.

Revision takes a great deal of effort, and is usually aided by reading
a poem out loud, sharing it with peers, and waiting a few days or weeks
for some objectivity.

We can think of revision in terms of minor and major repairs:

1. *Minor repairs* usually involve cutting and clarifying: cutting away the flat words, the clichés, the needless transitions, the vague abstractions; and clarifying the underdeveloped image, the under-nourished emotion, the unresolved situation.
2. *Major repairs* may involve the reworking of whole parts of the poem. There are no rules for this undertaking. The poet must imaginatively crawl back under the skin of his or her creation and attempt to vivify and develop those portions which are moribund and useless.

Finding an Audience

It is important to read one's poems out loud, to listen for the music and the clinkers. And it is wonderful to share these poems with others, to get feedback and encouragement. Inspiration comes from hearing others, experimenting with new themes or forms, finding models to imitate.

For the teacher of poetry, finding an audience means displaying and reproducing student poems, making them public for other students: bulletin boards, poetry readings, literary magazines, booklets of student poems. The poems as reflections of individual students become a means for students to connect with each other, mirrors that reflect in two directions.

The poems, first written in solitude, become instruments of communication and community.

References

Bachelard, Gaston. 1971. *The Poetics of Reverie*. Translated from the French by Daniel Russell. Boston: Beacon Press.

Housman, A. E. 1944. *The Name and Nature of Poetry*. New York: Macmillan.

Keen, Sam, and Anne Valley Fox. 1973. *Telling Your Story: A Guide to Who You Are and Who You Can Be*. New York: New American Library.

Milne, A. A. 1925. *The House at Pooh Corner*. Toronto: McClelland & Stewart.

Sexton, Anne. 1976. "From 1928 to Whenever: A Conversation with Anne Sexton." In *American Poets in 1976*. Edited by William Heyen. Indianapolis: The Bobbs-Merrill Company, Inc.

Stein, Jean, ed. 1956. "William Faulkner: An Interview." *Paris Review* (Spring). (Reprinted in *William Faulkner: Three Decades of Criticism*, edited by Frederick J. Hoffman and Olga W. Vickery. New York: Harcourt, Brace & World, Inc., 1963.)

Turco, Lewis. 1986. *The New Book of Forms: A Handbook of Poetics*. Hanover and London: University Press of New England.

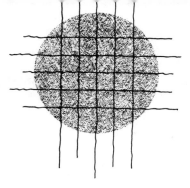

II Weaving the World

Introduction to Part II

We begin Part II with the awareness that we write in order to make sense out of this vast, multitudinous world, and eventually to make a home here. Writing shapes experience; experience feeds our writing. Rilke describes the spectrum of this dialogue:

> For the sake of a single verse, one must see many cities, men and things, one must know the animals, one must feel how the birds fly and know the gesture with which the little flowers open in the morning. One must be able to think back to roads in unknown regions, to unexpected meetings and to partings one had long seen coming; to days of childhood that are still unexplained, to parents whom one had to hurt when they brought one some joy and one did not grasp it (it was a joy for someone else); to childhood illnesses that so strangely begin with such a number of profound and grave transformations, to days in rooms withdrawn and quiet and to mornings by the sea, to the sea itself, to seas, to nights of travel that rushed along on high and flew with all the stars. . . . One must have memories of many nights of love . . . of the screams of women in labor. . . . But one must also have been beside the dying, must have sat beside the dead in the room with the open window and the fitful noises. (26–27)

We need a place to begin, a place out of which and from which we might view the world and begin the process of reconnecting the fragments of our experience, making a whole again, making us whole again. Metaphorically, we need to find the center: the center of our selves, the center of our culture.

The center provides a perspective from which the rest of the world makes sense, where the apparent chaos of everyday events slowly falls into place, gaining a coherence and lasting meaning.

Where is the center of the United States? Where is the center of our culture? Where is the center of me, the individual? We must look not only for the geographical center, the physical center, but the spiritual center, the heart that makes the rest of the body tick, the creative source of energy and direction.

Circles of Relationship

The materials of part II are arranged in a series of circles which spread out from the individual—the Me—at the center. To my ear, *me* is a stronger, more emphatic word than *I*. Ask a bunch of little kids which ones want some free candy, and you'll hear a chorus of "Me! Me! Me! Me!" Thus we put Me in the middle (Fig. 1).

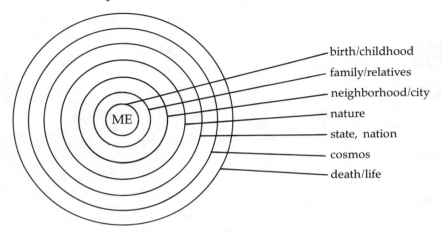

birth/childhood
family/relatives
neighborhood/city
nature
state, nation
cosmos
death/life

Figure 1. Starting from the egocentric self, we can reach progressively further outward to explore our relationship to different aspects of reality, and to deal with questions of universal significance.

We could add other circles such as "religion" and "ethnicity." But basically we have the Me—its origins, characteristics, and needs—and then the possible relationships which are also part of the identity of Me. I am an individual, but I am also my relationships.

The writer Sam Gill once went to hear Indian elders in southern Arizona discuss public education programs for Indians. He describes an old Papago man who rose and spoke slowly with great dignity and certainty:

> He began with the creation of the Papago world, by telling how Earthmaker had given the Papago land its shape and character. He identified the features of that creation with the land on which he had always lived, as had his father and all his grandfathers before him. Pausing in his story he asked how many of us could locate our heritage so distinctly. Then he went on to tell the stories of Iitoi, a child born in the union of earth and sky, who had acted as protector and teacher of the Papago under the name Elder Brother.

He told of the life of the Papago people, a way of life they have always enjoyed. (6)

The man spoke for about fifteen minutes in this manner before addressing the particular issues at hand. His intent was to establish a context:

> He was demonstrating to his audience a basic principle in education: knowledge has meaning and value only when placed within a particular view of the world. He was utilizing the way of his people by consulting the stories of the creation for the proper perspective from which to speak. There was power in his words and his statement was convincing. (6–7)

With the second part of *Word Weaving*, we begin a journey into relationships, and we ride on the back of language. Simon Ortiz says it well:

> I never decided to become a poet. An old-man relative with a humpback used to come to our home when I was a child, and he would carry me on his back. He told stories. My mother has told me that. That contact must have contributed the language of myself.... [T]he language of a person is a road from inside himself to the outside, and from that outside of himself to inside.... I write for myself, my parents, my wife and children, for my community of kinfolk, that way of life. I must do that to ensure that I have a good journey on my way back home and in order that it will continue that way. (174)

The poem, then, becomes a journey connecting one thing to another, perhaps like a serpent moving side to side, or like a spider in a gossamer web. It is certain that we will encounter detours, back alleys, new vistas, surprise turns in the road, potholes—all the turtles crossing the highway, all the forgotten trails left out of the AAA Guidebook.

Periodically we lose the way and become discouraged; periodically the world seems to fall apart and head for disaster. All of us who care for life on this planet must illuminate the paths, put braces to the wreckage, and spread buckets of plaster along the crack in the dam.

At the same time, pieces of the world are continually being born, coming into view, changing colors, emerging from the womb dripping with blood and water, breaking into the light from the birth sac. And poets must christen this perennial process, giving names to new beings and celebrating all the new transformations.

It is impossible for most of us to construct an intellectual, scientific framework that encompasses all of reality, but we are capable of making connections, of following the threads of the imagination which bind one thing to another—the process of weaving our lives into a creative vision of the whole. When this happens in the following poem by Pat Smith, the result is a celebration of being:

Walking the Arroyo
(for Bill Bishop)

Walking
down a dry wash like a crooked hallway
bent cloister in the earth
earth walls headhigh or more, red
and pitted like an empty switchboard:
holes for old root-systems
rotted out.

Somewhere above my head
it is the lemon-bitter prairie, it is February,
down here no month, no life, every time
and I can only follow you, your voice around the bends,
walking where water ran across a sandstone floor.
My feet sink, slip sometimes in lemon grass
dry-blown down here, and soft,
enough for a manger
(no rabbits, lizards even, to bed down).

And then down here, look down,
dark wallstain at my waist.
I think: blood wood meal bone
and bend to touch.
Soft carbon coming off the rock and clay
in dark smears on my thumb.

Firepit: charcoal, and a little bone.
We are walking where their fire was,
burned. Burned out. And they moved on,
walking the prairie, stalking down the sun.
Their shadows lengthened, shadows stretching out
to blend, at length, into the rolling dark.
My shoulders twitch: "Goose walking on your grave,"
my grandmother would say. And she is dead.

This is the place full of where things once were:
roots, water, fire. Men.

And all at once, dead charcoal in my hand,
I'm running hard, and stumbling to catch up,
I am filling the arroyo, gigantic I,
a cosmos swarms between this head, these feet,
how can I say how beautiful we are,
but words, immense, are blooming in my mouth:
Listen, I want to say,
                You are, I am.

                                —Patricia Clark Smith

References

Gill, Sam D. 1977. "The Trees Stood Deep." *Parabola* 2, no. 2 (Spring).

Ortiz, Simon. 1974. "Notes by the Contributors." In *The Man to Send Rain Clouds: Contemporary Stories by American Indians,* edited by Kenneth Rosen. New York: Vintage Books.

Rilke, Rainer Maria. 1949. *The Notebooks of Malte Laurids Brigge.* Translated by M. D. Herter Norton. New York: W. W. Norton & Company.

5 Origins

As humans we are endlessly curious about the question of origins. How did it all begin? When did it happen? Who made the earth? Which things were made first? Where did I come from? We ask about origins because we are an inquisitive species, anxious to extend our knowledge, and because origins give us a sense of identity and purpose. The question of *whence* shapes our questions of *how* and *why*.

A number of basic images are associated with the creation of the cosmos: sky, earth, air, fire, water, egg, darkness. Our personal origins begin with birth experiences, childhood rites, and names.

Sky and Earth

The imagination works overtime when we are out in the country staring at the moon and stars. People from all ages have wondered about the immensity of the night sky and have asked questions about the universe, time, and space. Often with stargazing comes the first experience of awe—a stronger experience than wonder. Awe involves mystery, the inexplicable, the grand and powerful. When in awe, we vacillate between feelings of personal inconsequence and the marvel of being a part of such a vast cosmos.

Robinson Jeffers attributes nature's grandeur to "The Excesses of God":

> Is it not by his high superfluousness we know
> Our God? For to be equal a need
> Is natural, animal, mineral: but to fling
> Rainbows over the rain
> And beauty above the moon, and secret rainbows
> On the domes of deep sea-shells,
> And make the necessary embrace of breeding
> Beautiful also as fire,
> Not even the weeds to multiply without blossom
> Nor the birds without music:
> There is the grand humaneness at the heart of things,
> The extravagant kindness, the fountain
> Humanity can understand, and would flow likewise
> If power and desire were perch-mates.

Origins involve much more than just prehistorical facts; origins involve attitudes and beliefs.

Most creation stories from the world's religions have regarded sky and earth with wonder, gratitude, and fear. Earth and sky are the twin sources of bounty and power, and it makes sense that the major gods and goddesses have been associated with aspects of one or the other.

Food and drink, as well as the destruction of floods and earthquakes, come from the earth. Powers under the earth are related to the origins of life and the mystery of death, as symbolized by the cycle of planting and harvesting. The seed in the earth sprouts, matures, and is harvested, just like the child who emerges from its mother's womb, grows, and dies. For ancient peoples the earth was alive, and she bountifully provided the food of life for all the creatures living on her.

The sky is associated with the powers of the sun, wind, rain, and lightning—forces capable of either destruction or creation. Early humans looked up and wondered about the daily passage of the sun across the sky. They looked at and dreamed about the patterns of stars which moved in cycles through the seasons, the waxing and waning of the moon, the tiny pinpoints of light which receded into great hollows in the darkness.

The moon in particular has been a source of mystery, stimulating poems and stories. Most cultures think of the moon as feminine and the sun as masculine, but some see a rabbit on the face of the moon, while others see a woman weaving, an elephant jumping off a cliff, or a girl with a basket on her head. Our idea of "the man in the moon" probably originated with the belief that the rays of the moon could fertilize the earth, that moonbeams were responsible for pregnancies. An anthropomorphic moon makes an appearance in "Autumn," by T. E. Hulme:

Autumn

A touch of cold in the Autumn night
I walked abroad,
And saw the ruddy moon lean over a hedge
Like a red-faced farmer.
I did not stop to speak, but nodded;
And round about were the wistful stars
With white faces like town children.

Macrocosm and Microcosm

Stories about creation and creativity inevitably use metaphors or analogies. The Chinese say that a primal sculptor, Pan Ku, chiseled the universe into shape, giving form to what was originally a chaotic lump of raw material. In like manner, the Hebrew Yahweh, in Genesis, formed Adam from clay. Followers of the Orphic religion in ancient Greece envisioned a primordial silver egg floating in space; from it Love hatched and was the basis for the rest of creation. Polynesians say that in the beginning Father-Sky lay on Mother-Earth and their children had to pry them apart with a cosmic tree and firmly position it to keep sky and earth from collapsing into each other again (see Charles Long, *Alpha*).

Metaphors are a way for us to envision the mysteries of creation. Dylan Thomas captures the wondrous first spark of life in lines from "In the Beginning":

> In the beginning was the mounting fire
> That set alight the weathers from a spark,
> A three-eyed, red-eyed spark, blunt as a flower;
> Life rose and spouted from the rolling seas,
> Burst in the roots, pumped from the earth and rock
> The secret oils that drive the grass.

As humans, we also want to belong to the created world, to feel a sense of identity with it, a task which is facilitated by the use of *analogy*. The four basic elements of earth, air, fire, and water, which are the building blocks of the cosmos (the macrocosm), relate to the individual human body (the microcosm).

Flesh and bones are like the earth; blood flowing through veins is like water coursing in streams and rivers. Breath is like the wind. My life force—my body's heat—is like fire, the energy of combustion. The four basic elements are thus both inside and outside. Ancient peoples found a sense of wholeness and continuity in the correspondences between the small and the large, the inside and the outside, the human body and the cosmos. A student makes a similar discovery:

> My beginning
> The beginning of everything
> The little bang
> The Big bang
> Water in my eyes shines
> Like the stars in space
> Tiny infant
> The universe

> —Kelly K./HS

The geography of the first creation also has its analogies. For example, mountains serve as places of mediation between earth and sky, where humans interact with sky deities such as Yahweh, on Mt. Sinai, and

Zeus, on Mt. Olympus. These high places correspond to our minds or spirits. Caves and canyons, which are entrances into the underworld, slash into the earth and make contact with the mother goddess. They represent entrances into the depths of our own psyches. Birds (and other feathered beings, such as angels) serve as messengers from earth to sky and symbolize aspiration and communication with the deities above. Snakes, in contrast, are the primary messengers from the earth to the underworld and symbolize psychic energy, especially as it travels along the spine.

At the center of this world is the garden, the paradise with a tree in the center: the place where peace and prosperity reign, where there is abundance and harmony. This corresponds to the lush, hidden garden within. The roots of the tree reach into the underworld, and its trunk and branches reach into the sky, effecting a reconciliation between the three dimensions: sky, earth, and underworld, or head, heart, and subconscious. In Hindu thought the tree represents the spine, the foundation of consciousness, along which the kundalini snake travels.

Surrounding these primordial lands is the wilderness, the region of monsters and chaos, the place of deserts and badlands which lies on the other side of the mountains, on the other side of the sea. Around all of it are the oceans, the edge of the world. It was from the primordial waters of chaos, after all, that the world was first born, as we are born out of our mothers' waters.

The old mythological stories are like a primer of essential images and metaphors which still may be used for imaging the primordial structure and energies of the external world and for exploring the creative process within.

Life began when lightning
struck a rock in the desert,
releasing the trapped gasses
inside.

First man was half horse and
half bird.
He flew when he was
happy...
walked when he was
tired...
and ran when he was
scared...

First woman was a poet
with a voice sweet as
an angel's humming.

Beauty began when the three
came together in harmony.

—Tom M./JH

I am a glob of clay
with bamboo veins
and Kool-ade blood
with wooden bones
and eyes of grapes
and teeth of stones.
If I am God's image
the mirror must be
CRACKED.

—Tim D./JH

Sometimes Beginnings Are Blue

When my sister was born
She was blue.
They say she almost died
From an umbilical cord wrapped around her neck.

My birth wasn't nearly as exciting.
It left such a minor impression on me
I can't remember it.

My little brother wasn't blue.
But his beginning is worth noting
Because his beginning was an end.
He had a hole in his heart,
And he died.

My mom had a hole in her heart, too,
After he died.
A hole of beginnings—and ends.

—Jennifer P./HS

Melissa at 5 Years

Melissa warms a brown egg
Between her palms, close to her lips
Cold from a carton,
Chosen one from the dozen.

It is the center now of a sphere
of kitchen towels in a drawer
Next to an Amish cookbook
Next to the oven's white side.

For three weeks at 3:15
Melissa will breathe on that egg
Held between her lifelines
Against her grape stained lips.
She anticipates the birth
Although brown eggs, her mother says
Can't hatch.

But at 5, Melissa
Has a good ear for heartbeats.
Sidewalk cracks cry
When her tennis shoe touches them,
The lava chips that embroider
The yard have names,
And a brown egg is throbbing
In the cup of her hand.

—Demetria L. M./C

Creating a Human Being

A family tree needs roots: parental roots, ethnic and religious roots, neighborhood and early schooling roots. It is not an accident of language that the word *roots* means one's ancestry as well as that part of the tree which grips the earth, anchoring trunk and branches. People cut off from their roots often seem cut off from purpose and direction.

Like a seed planted in the earth, we humans begin life in darkness, the primal darkness of the womb. We are like sea creatures, beings of the deep, surrounded by darkness and water. Using these images, we can begin to probe the mysteries of life itself. To return to our origins is to court the darkness within, to slowly sink into it. To plumb the depths of our beginnings is to immerse ourselves in water, to feel those places where water merges with darkness. It is also to find the pain associated with birth:

Congratulations

They were in the back seat of a car
New Year's Eve, 1969
I guess they were in love
It was a shotgun wedding

I was the bullet that seared
Into the flesh of their youth
For nine months the wound festered
My mother cried as the doctor washed pus from my limbs.

—Renee B./HS

Most children can listen again and again to stories about their origins: growing in mother's stomach, the birth process, learning to eat, to smile, to walk—all of the firsts in a baby's life. These stories satisfy needs for identity and self-affirmation. Baby stories are often exciting mini-dramas, filled with anticipation, crises, and resolutions. And within the family they can be endlessly repeated without boredom.

An Introduction

My dad sobbed in my mother's lap: I was born.
He wanted a girl more than the world.

Three brothers were reckless and rough;
But his little girl was a godsend, a miracle.

My frail mother smiled at her husband and new
     daughter.
Tears of joy introduced me to the world.

—Karen A./HS

The winter of the year I was born was a cold one in Minnesota; the snow lay thick and white and covered everything, and as it fell it buried the world anew each day. The houses were covered, the streets were white, even my father's car disappeared beneath a mountain of snow and had to be dug out each morning. The world was frozen into an icy, white stillness. Inside the houses, however, life moved; there were warm pockets of light and heat beneath the frozen snow-blanket. My father always demanded plenty of fresh air in the house; he was a robust giant, an active man who loved the elements. Every night the windows were thrown open for healthy, sound sleeping, and the cold winter air would enter the house and push the heat into corners or beneath blankets. And the baby boy, why, he needed that cold fresh air, make him a man . . . "No son of mine is going to . . . !" So the window in my room was left wide open, nothing but a screen between me and the freezing night. My mother thought it would be too cold, but no, no, he could take it. He had to.

In the morning my mother entered the room, and started with surprise. The bed seemed empty, no baby's head lay on the pillow, the boy had disappeared! Then she saw a thin wisp of something on the pillow sprouting like prairie grass from deep within the blankets. The boy had sunk into his blankets during the cold night, and nothing but a wisp of his hair could be seen.

—Mike G./C

Rites of Childhood

Childhood rites include the birth experience, cutting the umbilical cord
and disposing of it, bathing, naming, nursing and feeding, and presen-
tation to family and community. Mathilde Stevenson describes an
unusually beautiful ceremony used by Zuni Indians for presenting a
baby to the sun:

> On the morning of the tenth day the child is taken from its bed
> of sand . . . and upon the left arm of the paternal grandmother is
> carried for the first time into the presence of the rising sun. To the
> breast of the child the grandmother carrying it presses the ear of
> corn which lay by its side during the ten days; to her left the mother
> of the infant walks, carrying in her left hand the ear of corn which
> lay at her side. Both women sprinkle a line of sacred meal,
> emblematic of the straight road which the child must follow to win
> the favor of its gods. Thus the first object which the child is made
> to behold at the very dawn of its existence is the sun, the great ob-
> ject of their worship, and long ere the little lips can lisp a prayer
> it is repeated for it by the grandmother. (546)

Names

A name is usually the first gift for a child—after the gift of life itself.
A name provides a separate identity for the baby, but it also is a connection to family, tribe, nation, and religion. A child might need several
names for different stages in his or her development. Some children
have secret names, known only to family or secret society.

A name has power because it expresses something about who or what
an individual is. Saying a person's name will bring him or her to mind.
Some go further and believe that a name can actually invoke the person or being: say the word "Devil" and he might appear. The names
of the dead are never mentioned by Australian aborigines for fear of
invoking their ghosts and stirring up sad memories. On the other hand,
the names of the dead might be given to infants as a way of reincar-
nating a parent or grandparent.

Parents choose names from sources such as family names, the Bible,
TV, movies, and famous historical figures. How important are names
in shaping an individual's character? The Hebrew name David means
"beloved"; Martha means "lady"; Adam comes from *adamah*, meaning
earth or soil. A Hispanic neighbor's name is Jesús Maria, after a famous
mother and son. Although it is common in Mexico to name a son Jesús,
the Catholic Church north of the border discourages the use of that

name. Some names are tainted by history and would rarely or ever be chosen by a parent: Judas is one of these.

Are kids given the names of movie stars as a kind of boost toward a career? Some surnames point to particular occupations, like Painter, Carpenter, and Smith. Aptonyms are surnames which turn out to be incredibly apt: William Toothaker is a California dentist, Jeff Float was on the 1984 Olympic swim team, and Larry Speakes was a spokesperson for former president Ronald Reagan. Other names are bestowed as an honor, and provide both power and purpose, as John Fire Lame Deer explains,

> Each Indian name has a story behind it, a vision. . . . We receive great gifts from the source of a name; it links us to nature, to the animal nations. It gives power. . . . Take our famous chief Man-Afraid-of-His-Horse. It sounds funny in English. Man-Afraid once led the warriors in battle against the enemy who fled before him. The medicine men wanted to honor him and so they bestowed this name on him, which really means: He is so brave, so feared, that his enemies ran away when merely seeing his horse, even if he is not on it. That is a powerful name. He had to live up to it. (117)

Traditionally, a Navajo introduces himself or herself in terms of relationships to family and the mother's clan: so-and-so is son of Tall Woman of the Gray-Earth-Place clan. These relationships are fundamental to identity: "The worst that one may say of another person is, 'He acts as if he didn't have any relatives.' Conversely, the ideal of behavior often enunciated by headmen is, 'Act as if everybody were related to you' " (Kluckhohn, 100).

In the United States, slaves commonly were given the names of their owners; most names of blacks therefore do not link them to an African ancestry but to former slave owners, and painful memories. Because of this the Black Muslim movement promoted name changes: Malcolm Little became Malcolm X; Cassius Clay changed his name to Muhammad Ali; Lew Alcindor became Kareem Abdul-Jabbar. At Ellis Island, thousands of immigrants had their names changed. The old-world names were too complicated for the officials who processed new arrivals, so they arbitrarily assigned the immigrants easier, more "American" names. Other immigrants, like my grandfather, simply decided that they wanted more American names and changed them. At one time it was the practice at Bureau of Indian Affairs schools to rename Native American students who arrived fresh off the reservation, part of the effort to "acculturate" them to mainstream American society.

Increasingly in the United States people are known by their numbers: social security number, credit card numbers, driver's license number. In the 1960s people protested that it was demeaning to be a number rather than a person. One doesn't hear protests about this anymore; it's accepted. Once you were as good as your name; now you're as good as your credit rating.

My Name

I don't want to know where my name came from,
why my parents chose it. I think of
my name as medieval, strong,
aristocratic. Don't tell me otherwise.

How many mouths even now form it
on tongues, in love or in hate? Do you wonder at
my name? My vital organ? No,
don't ask it of me, you have your own.

—Robert M./HS

If I Had a Daughter

What would I name her?

Not Elizabeth, surely.
   (A venerable name, rippling across
   the centuries,
      but a white name . . . grey . . . no color at all.)

Audrey?
Or Charlotte?
(Names the warm
color of cocoa.)

Elaine, translucent . . .
green as leaves
in the first days of April.

Or Karen,
   the green
   of avocados under water.

Alice?
The rose-pink
of a rhubarb stalk.

Alyssa, white as alyssum?

No.
My child would cry out for a purple name:

Laura, black-purple of grapes and plums;
Julie, liquid violet.
Or Margaret,
that perfect shade of light purple,
a little darker than lilacs.

But what if she dreamed of a tawny name?

Then I would call her Andrea.

Andrea, color of noonday.

Color of the vase
in Van Gogh's "Sunflowers."

—Jeanne Shannon

Classroom Activities

Discussion Questions

1. What are some words associated with beginnings (words like *seed, egg, water, atoms*)? If you were a god, how would you create the world? How would it be different from the present one?

2. Are you creative? (This is a more difficult question for adults than for children. Adults find it easier to think in terms of work or productivity. But creativity can be found in a broad range of activities: gardening, cooking, sewing, decorating, woodworking—even conversation. How are these activities creative?)

3. What feelings do you have for the sun, for the moon, for the stars? Can you imagine the sun or moon being alive? (See "Autumn" by T. E. Hulme.) Is there any part of nature that is so large or powerful that it seems alive?

4. Early humans probably discovered fire through accident, perhaps by witnessing lightning strike a tree and set it aflame. Having discovered fire, they then set about to develop ways to use and control it. How do you suppose other natural events or processes came to be developed and utilized by humans? (Examples include agriculture, music, pottery, and weaponry.) Compare the responses to this question with those given for activity 2 in "Writing Suggestions."

5. Have you imagined your own birth? What do you think it was like? Did you exist before you were born?

6. Have you witnessed the birth of an animal, such as a cat or a dog? What happened?

7. The first human being on earth might have been like the figure of Ta'aroa in the Polynesian creation myth (see p. 7). Ta'aroa drifted around the cosmos in an egglike sphere until one day he broke out of the shell and wondered whether he was alone. Imagine that you are the very first human on earth.

8. What is the history behind your name? How do you feel about it? Did you ever use an alternate name?

9. One test of the appropriateness of your name is whether friends use it or whether they create a nickname for you. Where do nicknames come from?

10. Why do some women change their names when they marry? The Spanish culture provides for joining the last two names of the married couple: for example, Ortega y Gasset. Are there other ways to deal with names in marriage?

Writing Suggestions

1. Write a fantastic account of creation. (Some young poets start with "Under the bed," "In a big shoe under an odor eater," "When two people met in Wendy's under a bun," "Under the roots of an oak tree," or "In a tin cup.")

2. People in ancient times (and in the few remaining tribal societies today) used myths and other stories to make sense of their world, including dealing with some very basic questions—for example, the origin of fire. The Greeks tell a story about Prometheus stealing fire from the gods to give to the human race. Make up a mythical story to explain the origin of food, or of death, or any number of basic necessities or facts of life.

3. There are many firsts associated with infancy: first haircut, first tooth, first walk, first pair of shoes, and so forth. What "firsts" from your own life do you remember? (The stem "I remember when" can be repeated for each stanza of a poem.)

4. It is not easy to discover the inner me, the me within. Using metaphor and making associations with objects or animals can help: "I feel like a fist is closing around my stomach," or "Sometimes there is a bear inside, clawing to get out." What do you feel inside? "Inside I feel...."

5. There are several helpful phrases or stems that can lead into poems about your inner life; these stems can be repeated throughout the poem:

   Nobody knows ...   Inside I feel ...
   Hidden inside is a ...   They don't understand ...

6. Design a sandwich board (or a badge, a sign for your front yard, a headstone) that identifies who you are.

7. I can look at my own body, can watch parts of my body function, and yet I *am* my body; thus, it appears that I can be inside and outside my body at the same time. Is this possible? Write a poem directed at part of your body, describing how important this part is to you.

8. Use your name for an acrostic poem. For example,

Elephants
Lay for a
Long time
Every
Noon
　—Ellen D./JH

References

Hulme, T. E. 1924. *Speculations*. New York: Harcourt, Braceand Co.

Jeffers, Robinson. 1965. *Selected Poems*. New York: Vintage Books.

Kluckhohn, Clyde, and Dorothea Leighton. 1962. *The Navaho*. Garden City, N. Y.: Anchor Books.

Lame Deer, John Fire, and Richard Erdoes. 1972. *Lame Deer: Seeker of Visions*. New York: Simon and Schuster.

Long, Charles H. 1963. *Alpha: The Myths of Creation*. New York: George Braziller.

Stevenson, Mathilde Cox. 1962 [1887]. *The Religious Life of the Zuni Child*. 5th Annual Report of the Bureau of American Ethnology, Washington. (Reprinted in *American Indian Prose and Poetry*, edited by Margot Astrov. New York: Capricorn Books.)

Thomas, Dylan. 1963. *Miscellany*. London: J. M. Dent & Sons Ltd.

6 Family and Home

Historically around the world, the family and the home have been the basic social unit. We associate sustenance, nurturance, and unconditional love with the home and maternal images like the the nest, the cradle, and the hearth. The paternal qualities of home are shelter, security, and status: "A man's home is his castle."

In the most positive portrait, family and home provide a safe haven from a cold, harsh world, as well as a launching pad into the world for work and recreation:

> 'Mid pleasures and palaces though we may roam,
> Be it ever so humble, there's no place like home.
> (from John Howard Payne, "Home, Sweet Home")

In the nightmare version, the family engages in physical and psychological abuse, and the house or apartment (not a "home") is a place of anger, violence, and punishment—a kind of prison.

For most of us, family and home are the foundation upon which we build the rest of our lives; they provide a rich repository of images, feelings, impressions, and attitudes which either empower us toward creativity and the full expression of who we are, or cripple and inhibit our growth as human beings. Healthy writing radiates outward from this center.

Patriarchy, Matriarchy, and Partnership

In Western society the traditional family has been patriarchal: that is, a hierarchical structure with the father as head of the household and the rest of the family in a descending order through mother and the children according to age—with preference given to male children. A matriarchal family, in contrast, has a female as head of the household.

In the Middle Ages, the patriarchal hierarchy was seen to extend through nature, continuing downward through man and family to various orders of animals and birds to the least significant creatures on earth, such as insects. In like manner, the pattern extended upward

84

from the head of the household to various levels of male rulers to the ultimate patriarchal figure of God, often pictured as a grand old man with flowing white hair sitting on a celestial throne.

The design of this huge "chain of being" appealed to people, especially males, who needed clarity, order, and dominance; and, in fact, this male-dominated hierarchy seems to have been sanctioned, ages before, by both the Hebrew and the Greek religions.

For centuries the patriarchal model provided a workable pattern for family, church, and state, but it also produced conflict and rebellion. Such conflict is reflected in myths. At the center of Greek creation myths, for example, is the rebellion of the son against the father: the god Cronos, with the assistance of his mother, rebelled against his father Uranus (the sky) and castrated him. Cronos, in turn, after trying to swallow all his children, had a son named Zeus, who, aided by his mother, turned against his father and defeated him in battle. In the Bible are stories of Eve's rebellion; the conflict between Cain and Abel; the trickery of Jacob (with his mother's advice) against his brother, Esau; the rebellion of Absalom against his father, David. These patterns of conflict continue to the present day:

The Fight

There I was arguing with my little
brother
Suddenly I punch and he falls over
on his back
I notice that his face is red with
anger
Then with a flick of his wrist I
see he's throwing something at me
Through the air comes a pair of pliers
spinning end over end
My life passes before my eyes and I fall to the ground
just dodging it
I'm so lucky he has a crooked arm.

—Edward R./JH

As recently as a generation ago in rural America, the family had an economic as well as an emotional base: working hands, a shared purpose, and an endowment for the next generation. But the dynamics of the traditonal family are under attack today. An additional responsibility has been added in this new age: the family should provide a healthy and open environment in which individual members are able to fully develop their emotional and mental potentials as human beings. Wives as well as husbands? Children as well as parents? Girls as well as boys? YES!

We are in the midst of a massive, wrenching switch of the family pattern or paradigm—perhaps the most revolutionary change of the twentieth century. More and more people are thinking in terms of a partnership model for their primary relationships, rather than a patriarchal model. In such a relationship, the man and the woman are equal partners whose needs and desires are treated with equal respect and opportunity. Children in this relationship have a full voice in family affairs consistent with their physical and psychological needs, and are treated with respect and dignity as individuals. (For more on patriarchal, matriarchal, and egalitarian models, see *The Sword and the Chalice*, by Riane Eisler.)

The Modern Family: Conflict and Resolution

One wonders whether the family can survive the strains and pressures put on it by modern living and the shifting roles of men, women, and children.

We are driven back to basic definitions: what constitutes a family, anyway? A distinction is made between nuclear families (mother, father, and children) and extended families (parents, children, grandparents, and other close relatives). Today there are also single-parent families, single adoptive fathers, single adoptive mothers, mixed or combined families, unmarried couples living like married couples, and househusbands. Perhaps families should be defined by what is provided for its members. If a "family group" nurtures, comforts, and protects, then the concept of "family" should be extended beyond blood lines.

Since it is not absolutely clear how either the old patriarchal model or the new egalitarian models should function in a modern, urban society, family expectations inevitably conflict. Children need some guidelines to prevent chaos, but they also need to learn how to exist freely and openly within the family. Children need to participate harmoniously and lovingly within the family, yet also learn how to assert themselves competitively in a capitalist society.

We retain a kind of myth of the frontier for the maturation of children: they must go through a certain amount of rebellion at home in order to become separate and strong enough to survive in the wilds of the marketplace. A child may rebel over clothes, haircuts, smoking, drugs, sex, and many other things; and the parents either assert their control by drawing lines or they let go. The students in one class of mine made a list of things which were forbidden by their parents as they were growing up. Some restrictions were expected, such as swearing, playing doctor, and talking to strangers, but some were unique and even humorous:

French kissing: "Even the cows and the pigs in the barn don't do that."

Sitting on a boy's lap without using a telephone book for a cushion.

To cross my legs in my father's presence [listed by a girl].

To look at my body; it was a sin.

I was forbidden to read Alger Hiss.

When conflict in the home becomes excessive, family members leave: children run away, fathers leave, mothers leave, families break up:

Let's Talk

What to say
"It's a question of values"
"We are simply different"

"This is not communication.
The words simply promote
Reactions.
"Open your mind!"
"Say something real!"

"I don't see any point in continuing."
I am a restless voyager
frightened of ghosts.
I haven't lived at home
for eighteen years.

—Thomas A./HS

Numerous parents complain that raising their children is one of the most important challenges of this life, but one of the tasks they are least prepared for. There are, however, the success stories: parents and children who communicate with each other, respect each other, and help each other to grow and fulfill themselves.

My mother is like
a biscuit
warm, soft, crusty.
always nice
with butter and jam.

—Marc B./JH

My Family

My father is like a knife
he's cut a special place in
my heart
He's always carving new things
for me to do
He pokes me when I need it
and has a sharp mind
But he's always there to
protect me.

—Ronnie A./JH

Heart Pajamas

Dad,

Remember—

—those flannel pajamas with "MY HEART BELONGS
TO DADDY" printed on them?

—long baths and wrapping me in a big furry towel
afterwards?

—reading in your lap, my big easy chair?

—picking me up at Kim's house? 12:00. Scared.
Lonely. And too young to spend the night?

—Shopping? You would let me get anything I
wanted. Mom never did that.

—my science fair project? Or was it your project?

—you left for a year.

—When you came home, I had a boyfriend and a
driver's license.

—Karen A./HS

How Would You Like It, Dad?

Sarah has always believed a good offense
is the only defense.
Never admit you're wrong, never admit
defeat.

Stand there, toe to toe. Even with all
the evidence. Her room filled with dirty
clothes, the blank pages of a history paper,
the rabbit's empty food dish.

How would you like it, dad? she screams.
Well, how would you?

I wouldn't. But we play out our roles
anyway, to the end.
One a mirror image of the other.
Her eyes wet like mine.

—David Johnson

Homes Reflect Who We Are

All kinds of houses and apartments, all shapes and sizes, are made into "homes," places of rest, comfort, and enjoyment.

Some houses are built to stand out, to stand up and point at themselves and their occupants. If you travel across the great plains of Nebraska or the Dakotas you will see houses, barns, and silos that stand up; the grain elevators along the railroads are like small mountains on the plains.

In the Southwest you will find houses and whole villages made of adobe that blend into the landscape. The earth-colored dwellings merge with the background. It is not simply a question of using two different building materials—wood or brick on the one hand, and adobe on the other; it is also a matter of psychology, since houses are an extension of the people who live in them. Some people want to stand out, to be noticed, while others prefer to blend in, to be part of a group or part of a landscape: "Our house is our corner of the world. As has often been said, it is our first universe, a real cosmos in every sense of the word" (Bachelard, 4).

The spaces within the home also reflect the character of its inhabitants. Does everyone in the family have some private space? Are there special places where certain activities are carried out? I miss the attics of my youth, those confined places through which only a small, limber person could crawl and squeeze. My first home also had a coal cellar, where strange shadows stimulated my imagination.

Many homes have two main centers. The daytime center is the kitchen. Years ago it contained a hearth or fireplace, but today a stove with an oven is the central fixture of this room. Here at the very heart of the house is the fire used for cooking and warming the room. These essential benefits radiate outward to the rest of the house.

The nighttime center is the bedroom: a place of intimacy and inwardness, where we dream, make love, and rest. Our first world is the cradle in the middle of the bedroom, in the middle of the house, at the center of the cosmos: "Life begins well, it begins enclosed, protected, all warm in the bosom of the house" (Bachelard, 7).

In fact, the house is a perfect image of a person: from the head in the attic to the dark night of the soul in the cellar, from airy inspiration above to subterranean stirrings below. We must use our imaginations to explore all the metaphors waiting to be discovered in the house:

windows	chimneys
stairs	furnace
closets	insulation
hearth or fireplace	attic
cellar	bathtub or shower

These images and many others carry us back and forth from all the houses we have lived in to all the nooks and crannies of our own inner spaces.

Feeling at Home

A university class of returning teachers was given the following assignment: "Draw the floor plan of a house you lived in before you were twelve years old. Point out favorite places where special activities went on" (see Keen and Fox, 48). All of the floor plans were displayed around the classroom and discussed; a flood of memories came with these discussions.

The homes were generally similar to each other, with a living space within four walls and an occasional shrub or treehouse outside the back door. Then we came to a Navajo woman who had been raised in a hogan in Arizona. Her home had one room in the center with at least fifty feet of land around it. An outdoor kitchen under shade trees was used in the heat of the summer; other areas were for playing or resting. Her discussion of "home" opened everyone's eyes. It was as if urban life had forced the idea of home into the four walls of a house, while the Navajo felt at home in a larger space, which included nature.

The real issue is whether we feel at home when we're in our dwelling, for this is the standard by which we measure whether we feel at home in the world. We actually have a choice: to wander through life alienated and alone, treating the world as a separate object subject to our dominance and manipulation; or to make a home in this world, to belong to this world, to care for it and love it as an extension of ourselves.

Sterling, Colorado

"On Saturdays we would go to town
after picking potatoes all week
and the Anglos would laugh at us
and call us dirty Mexicans,"
my mother tells me

as she sits and crochets
surrounded by the red, white, and blue ribbons
won at the State Fair

A picture of John F. Kennedy
smiles from the wall

Her busy, brown hands
pull pulling the thread
from the spool on her carpet

A portrait of Jesus
stares from the wall

The needle flick flick flickering
as she loops the laughter
and pulls the thread, pulls the thread
as she loops the Saturdays
and pulls and pulls the thread
as she loops and loops the laughter
and Saturdays in Sterling
into yet another doilie

—Leroy Quintana

I remember my father with his pipe on the porch on cool summer nights, the orange of the coals and the smell like wood being
cut on the big saws in the basement, how the lights would dim—
perhaps it was this darkness that bleached his hair like the albino
cave snakes I have heard about. He bit his pipe hard when he yell-
ed and it wiggled like a needle pushing into the red. He sometimes
appeared to glow as he dozed in the blue light of our TV and moths
hurled themselves against the windows. His body might have
secreted chemicals when he bailed me out of jail. Or in 60 years
has white dust grown fond of him, embracing him as his children
never did? No, I suspect it has something to do with the banjo lean-
ing in the corner and fragments of a song, barely audible behind
the screeching saws with fading background vocals, "You shoulda
this, Don, you shoulda that."

—Carl P./C

Rooms in My House

1.
My brother's sank
        under the weight
of his submarines

Mine had generic walls
        covered with pictures of
        grown men wearing uniforms,
        throwing and catching
        a pure white ball.

I had a shelf with books;
        one book
for each player on the walls
and I would read everyday
        about
        hard work

I knew I shouldn't marry
   or smoke behind the gym
and I'd eat the right foods
and go to church every Sunday
   before the game.

2.
My father's den was warm
with its deer head and fireplace
and his chair, the old hi-fi
and his shelf, like mine
only thicker longer darker
and loaded down with mugs

There were mugs from Japan
   and the mug
   his comrades gave him
   and mugs
   he won at fairs
   and one mug
   from a lost war.

When my father dies
   I shall give his mugs
   to my brother;
he can use them to replace
   the submarines.

3.
No one was allowed in mother's
     living room.
It had white chairs and an exotic rug
from a Turkish tourist trap.

There was marble from Athens
and the whiteness must have been
from Norway.

The high ceilings made mother
   FEEL PROPER
when reading her Bible
   as did
the hint of sunshine through
   stained-glass
     curtains.

4.
There was no mixture of my parents
in their room.
   Mother's smell
   was in the corner.
Father either
slept or   hung drapes.
   But there were his
   magazines

laid face down in the tallest drawer
on top of his socks, folded so neatly
in Air Force blue;
awaiting inspection.
5.
There were no pets or treehouses.
We'd mow every Saturday
then wash all three cars
then hose down the garage
then neatly arrange our
   balls, bats and gloves.

And we were only allowed
to have one friend over
   at a time.

                 —Tanner P./C

Classroom Activities

Discussion Questions

1. Who are the important persons in your family? Do you have any black sheep? Heroes? Heroines? Is there someone who keeps the family together or someone who divides it?

2. What are your family traditions? Are there special cures for illness? Special sayings for particular occasions? Old jokes or old stories that are told and retold?

3. What is the difference between sustenance and nurturance?

Writing Suggestions

1. Make a list of three words ending in -*er* that describe you, such as *runner, reader,* and *achiever.* Make a list of three -*er* words that are not you. Discuss these qualities and write about them.

2. Do you have a family tree? If you don't, try to put one together with the help of relatives. As an additional or alternative project, make up an imaginary family tree. Who would you want to include? Are there fantasy characters that you would include?

3. The family is an endless source of writing materials. You might begin with family photos. Do the faces reveal or hide feelings? From the arrangement of people in the photo can you tell who is the boss in this family? Poems can be written with the stem "I remember when...."

I Remember When . . .
I first wrote my name
I locked myself in the closet
I broke my mom's high heel shoe
    and blamed it on my sister
My grandpa put me on his steam shovel
    and left me there for an hour
I was babysitting a 5 month old baby
    and locked myself out of the house
I burned my grampa's bus
I was dreaming I fell off a cliff
    but when I woke I had fallen off
    my bunk bed
I heard the legend of the killer deer
    with a rack of 23 points
I used to pull my mom's eyes
    open when she was asleep
                          —Group poem/JH students

4. Comparisons with ordinary objects can illuminate features of family members:

    My family is like a pencil sharpener,
    always grinding me down, to the way
    they want me.

    My mother is like an oil can.
    She is always able to fix
    those squeaky little problems
    we so frequently have.

                          —JH students

5. Sometimes it is difficult to relate to members of our family, to say what we mean. Write a letter to a member of your family and tell him or her the things that you've really wanted to say for some time. If someone has died before you had a chance to say important things, write a letter to that person and say those things now.

6. Design a "Help Wanted" sign for yourself. For example,

    HELP WANTED: In desperate need of counseling; need of attention, love, an open heart, and a listening ear when scared, lonely and insecure; No experience necessary; no charge; just someone to care with all strings attached.

                          —Karen A./HS

7. The home is a good place for creating lists of things: foods; games; objects in your closet, family room, or attic.

8. Draw the floor plan of the house you lived in as a child. Designate the important spaces in the house: play, work, meals, secrets, solitude. Write down important memories from this project.

9. Write about your home as a human being, or imagine yourself as an animal and describe your surroundings (lair, cave, nest, etc.).

References

Bachelard, Gaston. 1969. *The Poetics of Space.* Translated by Maria Jolas. Boston: Beacon Press.

Eisler, Riane. 1988. *The Chalice and the Blade: Our History, Our Future.* San Francisco: Harper & Row.

Keen, Sam, and Anne Valley Fox. 1974. *Telling Your Story: A Guide to Who You Are and Who You Can Be.* New York: New American Library.

Payne, John Howard. 1918. "Home, Sweet Home." In *I Hear America Singing.* Boston: C. C. Birchard & Co.

7 Love and Loving: Romance and Friendship

The images of love are so familiar; found on greeting cards and book jackets, they also sell all kinds of products through the media to the unwary and the lonely.

The mysterious center of human love is always the heart, often symbolized by the rose. The capricious power of love is portrayed in the figure of Cupid and his arrows. The gentleness of love is imaged in doves. Love's closeness or union is seen in the Chinese yin and yang symbol, interlocked hearts and circles, and clasped hands.

These images point to the process by which two separate beings are bonded together, reconciled or unified: *the mystery of two persons becoming one*. A cycle is completed when a new being is created out of this union, when a baby is born from the couple: *the mystery of one becoming two*. These unions and new births are not mysterious in physical terms: sexuality and parenting instincts are ubiquitous in the animal kingdom. But when we consciously move beyond a sense of ourselves as separate beings (our ego identities) and identify—even merge—with another person, we are involved in a deeply spiritual mystery.

Man and woman reach beyond their separateness to an intimate union; from this union a child is born. Parent and child are bonded together, and in the process of maturation an individual emerges and ventures into the world. Friend embraces friend, and from the strength of this relationship two people are empowered to more fully express their individuality.

Science can explain many things about humans and the natural world, but it cannot adequately interpret the fundamental mysteries associated with love. Yes, science can reduce love to hormones or libido, but these are partial descriptions. Ultimately, we cannot account for the powerful feeling that sends a mother back into a burning house to rescue her child, or drives a soldier to fall on a grenade to save his platoon. According to Erich Fromm, this human bonding is our most powerful drive:

> It is the most fundamental passion, it is the force which keeps the human race together, the clan, the family, society. The failure to achieve it means insanity or destruction—self-destruction or destruction of others. (18)

Romantic Love

The idea that man and woman originally came from a single primal being is widespread around the world. In the Genesis story, for example, Eve is born from Adam's rib. In his *Symposium*, the Greek philosopher Plato relates a myth about the origin of the sexes: at one time, males and females were united in a single person, but Zeus cut this person in half so that humans would turn their attention away from rebelling against the gods and turn instead to each other. Ever since then people feel incomplete alone, but when together, two people can feel a sense of wholeness. Obviously, these stories are not meant to be biological explanations of gender, but rather to point to the powerful attraction between partners.

Eros, the Greek god of love, was handsome but spoiled. For sport he shot his arrows of desire into both humans and gods, often causing problems between husband and wife. From Eros we get the word *erotic*, which means sexual desire. No doubt his arrows provided both husbands and wives excuses for flirtatious, adulterous behavior: "I was swept off my feet. . . . I don't know what came over me." Eros and Cupid, the Roman love god, remind us that love can forcefully strike anywhere and anytime.

One of the earliest lyric poets, and the first woman poet of renown in the West, is the Greek Sappho, who wrote about the antithetical passions associated with love in the seventh century B.C.:

> With his venom
>
> Irresistible
> and bittersweet
>
> that loosener
> of limbs, Love
>
> reptile-like
> strikes me down
>
> (Barnard, No. 53)

Historians tell us that our own age's romantic love had its roots in "courtly love," which arose in medieval times and celebrated the passionate love a knight had for his lady. In the scheme of courtly love, the lady was put on a pedestal. The knight's love, which fed on obstacles in a relationship, was demonstrated in his willingness to undertake dangerous deeds for his lady. From this period came the troubadour poets, who provided a model for crooners and sentimental seducers ever since.

More songs are piped over the airwaves about love than any other topic. A typical country and western song, for example, is about either getting or losing love, achieving bliss or healing a broken heart.

Hollywood and soap operas have also contributed to the basic ingredients of romantic love, to such things as love at first sight; ultimate and everlasting, irrational, perpetual ecstasy; total preoccupation with love and the loved one; the willingness to sacrifice anything for love and the loved one; a storybook marriage and a lifetime of happiness:

Crush

Painting my nails
Instead of math.
Curling my hair.
Practicing phrases
In front of a mirror,
Laughs, smiles, looks,
Seeing Dad too late.
Perfectly coordinating
Each daily event
To run into you,
To see you, and
Pretend that I didn't.
Gentle insanity
Possessing quickly
Its helpless victim.
And the worst of it is
I don't even know you!
(No, the worst of it is
You don't know me.)

—Jill O./HS

Couples that survive Cupid's arrows know that a lasting love relationship is accompanied by any number of day-to-day, mundane activities—like cooking, cleaning, sickness, in-laws, repairs, credit cards. Contact with these can quickly remove the glow from "falling in love." We like to say that infatuation is different from love. Infatuation is associated with sexual chemistry and good vibrations, whereas mature love includes, in addition, friendship, patience, understanding, and care for the other person's spiritual growth:

A Decade

When you came, you were like red wine and honey
And the taste of you burnt my mouth with its sweetness.
Now you are like morning bread,
Smooth and pleasant.
I hardly taste you at all, for I know your savor;
But I am completely nourished.

—Amy Lowell

Are there things other than wine that become better with age, and thereby serve as metaphors for mature love?

As larger portions of our society become more mechanized and anonymous, more pressure will be placed on intimate relationships, and the breakdown of these relationships will be increasingly traumatic and tumultuous.

Many fine poems, however, have resulted from broken hearts. Young poets often begin to write out of feelings of loneliness and suffering. Expressing these feelings may bring about what the Greek philosopher Aristotle called a *catharsis*, an emotional purging or release of tension. Love involves conflicting emotions; the thin line between love's joys and love's pains can produce poetry.

Recipe for a Broken Heart

3 cups pain
2 tablespoons callousness
1/2 dozen Idontcares
1/4 teaspoon Ihateyou extract
pinch of gall*

Combine all ingredients in Ostracizer or conventional blender. Bake in a pre-heated discussion for too long. Keep chilled and unresponsive until serving.

*Amount may vary according to desired results. Suit to ugliness.

—Robert M./HS

So, you want to know
How to stop the pain
When your heart is shattered?

Well, first
forget.
Forget how it feels to be held.
Forget walking hand-in-hand along the beach.

Next, Remember.
Remember how it feels to wonder if he'll call.
Remember hating the way he told you
you wear too much make-up.

After you've finished
Forgetting and remembering,
Take a bubble bath
And go to bed.

—Caren L./HS

Cut Flowers
(On deciding to remain a virgin)

He was saying how virgins were diamonds
Because they are so rare.
"What are other women, then?"
"Oh, they're cut diamonds."

(I don't want to be chiseled.
Shaped to fit a certain man's design
Like some Pygmalion statue.
I'd rather discover my own facets,
Reveal my own inner colors,
Reflect my own desires.)

He was saying how I was a flower
He passed by each day.
How each day the desire to pick me grew.
How hard it was for him
To simply gaze and smell
But not touch.

(If I am a flower,
Are other women cut flowers?
Are past lovers simply arranged
In a vase of your past?
I don't want to be plucked.
Placed on your shelf
To gather dust with the others.
I'd rather continue to grow and blossom
In my own bed
Than wither and fade
In yours.)

—Carla W./C

Qualities of Friendship

In Greek there are different words for different kinds of love; knowing
the difference helps to keep relationships sorted out. The Greek word
for friendship love, for example, is *philia*. (Philadelphia has its roots in
this word: *philia* = *love, adelphos* = *brother*; thus, the city of brotherly
love.)

Once a new family moved in across the street. They had a four-year-
old daughter and so did we. First the two girls just eyed each other
from their yards. Soon they got together and one of them said, "Bet
I can lift you!" And the other said, "Oh yah?! Bet I can lift you too!"
And so they took turns lifting each other off the ground. After that they
became close friends.

Friends are so important that we create little rituals to find ways to intially develop friendships, and then to test them to make sure our friends are really trustworthy and loyal. When I was a kid we became "blood-brothers" by pricking or nicking our wrists and then holding them together. This was the closest bond we knew, outside the family. Little did we know that this act was based on a very old tradition of blood covenants, which were more binding than food or salt covenants since they involved mingling the essence of life, blood.

> You know you have a friend
> When you lift each other up to see who weighs more
> When you swap girls for a day just to see what they say
> You no longer have a friend
> When you knock each other down to see who hurts more
> When you steal each other's girls out of spite
>
> —Eliot S./HS

You can really talk to a friend, tell your friend anything, confess anything. You can tell things to a friend that you might not—would not—even tell your parents. But not just talk. A friend is a companion who helps carry your burdens through thick and thin. Somewhere a maxim states, "You will know your true friends when the going gets tough."

Veterans returning from combat describe the ultimate expression of friendship: personal sacrifice. Every war has its tales of heroism when a soldier risks his life for his buddies. In the New Testament book of John are the words "Greater love hath no man than this, that a man lay down his life for his friends."

Models for Friendship

Two famous pairs of friends from the Old Testament are Ruth and Naomi, and David and Jonathan.

After the death of her husband and two sons, Naomi decides to return from Moab to the country of Judah. She advises each of her daughters-in-law to return to their original homes, but Ruth replies in words that ring of devotion and loyalty:

> Do not press me to leave you and to turn back from your company, for
>
> wherever you go, I will go,
> wherever you live, I will live.
> Your people shall be my people,
> and your God, my God.

Where you die, I will die
and there I will be buried.
May Yahweh do this thing to me
and more also,
if even death should come between us!

(Ruth 1:16–17, *Jerusalem Bible*)

The story of David and Jonathan depicts a friendship that is deeper than body or mind. The Book of Samuel says, "The soul of Jonathan was knit to the soul of David, and Jonathan loved him as his own soul." When Jonathan is killed, David laments,

O Jonathan, in your death I am stricken,
I am desolate for you, Jonathan my brother.
Very dear to me you were,
your love to me more wonderful
than the love of a woman.

(II Samuel 1:26, *Jerusalem Bible*)

Is it possible that love between two people of the same sex can be deeper than love between two persons of the opposite sex? It was common in the Greek tradition to prize love between two men. From Homer comes the story about Achilles and Patroclus in the *Iliad*. After Patroclus is killed, Achilles reenters the war with Troy and avenges Patroclus, killing many Trojans. It is said that the bones of the two friends were buried together, and that with the other heroes of the Trojan War they are immortals together on the White Island in the Black Sea.

We were really good friends.
We wanted to marry.
We spent hours in front of a toy shop,
To choose our daughter
    from the thousands in the window.
"I like the blue one."
And every day we had a new child
And a new name.
Our partings, in front of my house,
    returning from the park, were terrible.
We hugged each other for a long time.
And our mothers laughed
    we were only five.

—Guilia C./HS

"Maureen's Friend"

I hate You.
I trusted You, and told You everything:
My crush on Your brother,
My dream of being a pilot,
My first kiss,
And You told Maureen everything.
I hate You.

—Dee H./HS

I didn't ask for your opinion
And I don't want to discuss it
Mind your own business
And stay out of mine
There's only one thing left for me to say
When you don't do as I ask:
Thanks for being a friend.

—Aviva B./HS

All alone again
no one to talk to
no one to listen to
all alone once again.

—Martha B./JH

Loving the World

Love plays so many important roles on this earth. The first time we fall in love as a young person something magical happens to the world: it begins to glow and resound with music. The birds sound beautiful and the flowers look stunning. We feel like skipping down the walk and doing extra favors for sisters and brothers. Love for another person seems to radiate outward, allowing us to see beauty in other things. A sense of well-being, a feeling of appropriateness, a warm coloration of experience—these become the standard by which we measure the effects of love.

Love can be a kind of lens or window through which we view the world and discover its vibrancy and beauty. Malcolm Muggeridge describes such a perspective when after a long absence in Russia he was reunited with his wife and two sons in Switzerland:

Such moments of happiness, looked back on, shine like beacons, lighting up past time, and making it glow with a great glory.

Recollecting them, I want to jump up and shout aloud in gratitude at having been allowed to live in this world, sharing with all its creatures the blessed gift of life. Alienation is to be isolated and imprisoned in the tiny dark dungeon of the ego; happiness is to find the world a home and mankind a family, to see our earth as a nest snugly perched in the universe, and all its creatures as fellow-participants in the warmth and security it offers. . . . So, such moments of happiness comprehend a larger ecstasy, and our human loves reach out into the furthermost limits of time and space, and beyond, expressing the lovingness that is at the heart of all creation. (269–70)

First Love

She's the only one
he allows on his motorbike,
and she knows it.

Something older
than her fourteen years
tells her how to toss her head,
her dark hair falls like a shadow
down her back.

You can see the new moon
in her smile
as she drives past.

—David Johnson

An Armadillo Is the Loneliest Man in the World

If you love me, why do you bitch at me?
    Because I love you.
Why do you try to run my life?
    Because I love you.
Why do you let me take advantage of you?
    Because I love you.

If you love me, why are you so possessive?
    Because I don't want to lose you.
But you won't
    I'm terrified
Don't be, I love you too.
    Why?
An armadillo is the loneliest man in the world.

—David W./HS

Mother

Morning like a cluttered memo board
So many things to do, to be, to follow.
Dragged down in the fishbowl of this small town
Safe in the cocoon of motherly love.
My most lenient critic, in a plaid robe and a genuine smile.
My mother is a prism catching rays in the window,
The unmistakable feeling of a clean towel warm from the dryer,
The smell of beef stew in a big silver pot on the stove.
A spice rack,
A bandana and brown hands and knees from yardwork,
The neighbor who always has some eggs to loan,
A string of antique bells and a windchime,
A dish of potpourri and a tiny glass of amaretto,
A song by James Taylor,
The purse that always holds enough money for the gumball machine,
The perfect spot on a fluffed-up pillow,
The smell of a live Christmas tree,
A trusty push lawnmower and an acre of grass,
A housekey,
A funky red-brick house with a broken doorbell,
A soft and well-worn t-shirt,
The caretaker of my six feline siblings,
An unconditional love,
My friend.

—Christie M./C

Classroom Activities

Discussion Questions

1. Love is a strong emotion, like its opposite, hate. What experiences have you had with strong emotions? How have they affected your life?

2. How do we learn to love? Do we have to be taught to love?

3. Are there different kinds of love for different relationships? Different occasions? Can you love someone without liking them?

4. The -*ship* ending of *friendship* has its roots in the word *shape* and the idea of creating or shaping with one's hands. How do these ideas relate to friendship?

5. How do we make friends? How do we keep them?

6. What are the different stages in friendship? When you hear "This person knows me better than I know myself," what stage is that?

7. Listen to the lyrics in Simon and Garfunkel's "Bridge Over Troubled Waters." Is there someone who is a "bridge over troubled waters" in your life?

8. Is it more difficult to have a friend of the opposite sex? Does desire get in the way of friendship?

9. In 1936, Dale Carnegie's book *How to Win Friends and Influence People* was published, and it has been a best-seller ever since. It instructs business people and professionals in the techniques of super salesmanship. What kind of friends do you think Carnegie is talking about in the title?

10. At one time, it was customary to call a child born out of wedlock a "love-child." Is "love-child" preferable to "bastard" or "illegitimate"? If a child has a mother, how can he or she be called "illegitimate"?

11. Does the word *wedlock* (*wed* + *lock*) indicate something about how people used to view marriage (or still do)? Discuss both the positive and negative connotations of the word.

Writing Suggestions

1. True or false: the stronger you feel about a subject, the easier it is to write about it. Well, that sounds right. Feelings are like a head of steam: when they build up pressure, all you have to do is release the valve and write. Nevertheless, a blank sheet of paper can inhibit this process. One way to begin is to make lists: (a) What makes me really happy? (b) What makes me angry? (c) What makes me sad? Use these lists, along with metaphor and hyperbole, for longer pieces of writing.

2. Write a recipe for friendship.

3. So many songs are written about broken hearts and dreams. Conduct a brief survey of your favorite radio station by keeping track of the love messages. Write about your findings.

4. What kinds of remedies do you recommend for a broken heart? Make a list: long walks, reading a book, watching TV, shopping. Write about repairing a broken heart.

5. Write an imaginary "Dear Abby" letter and a reply to the letter.

References

Barnard, Mary, trans. 1958. *Sappho.* Berkeley: University of California Press.

Fromm, Erich. 1956. *The Art of Loving.* New York: Harper & Row Publishers.

Muggeridge, Malcolm. 1972. *Chronicles of Wasted Time: Part 1—The Green Stick.* London: Collins.

8 Food and Fiesta

Everyone must eat and drink to satisfy physical needs, but if food were simply a question of nutrition and basic food groups we would not concern ourselves with it in a book on poetry. In fact, various foods and beverages provide essential symbolic bridges between psychological, social, spiritual, and physical needs.

Primary foods such as bread, meat, honey, salt, milk, and wine reverberate with social and spiritual meanings. Conversely, the word *hunger*—and words linked to hunger, such as *desire, emptiness, appetite, yearn, ruminate,* and *crave,* remind us how we use the language of food to describe our emotional needs.

Feeding the Psyche

As babies, our first way to relate to the world is by eating. We begin life by tasting and testing reality with our mouths. The world is immediately divided into two parts: (1) the eatable and those who feed us, and (2) the non-eatable and those who don't—or can't—feed us. It is one of the early mysteries and supreme goods that mother is both eatable and non-eatable, and that we can satisfy both our desire for pleasure and our physical appetite from the same thing, the breast.

From the very beginning food is both biological and psychological: nursing and a full stomach bring feelings of security, closeness, communion, and peace. Our psyches are suspended along the alimentary canal.

As we grow, we continue to use words associated with eating and food to communicate psychological needs: the spirit hungers and thirsts; ideas are ingested or digested or chewed over; couples nourish or consume one another; some parents devour their children; large numbers of children are starving for attention.

Furthermore, one kind of hunger can be mistaken for another: a person might overeat trying to satisfy a psychological hunger or, on a subtler level, lust after material things, collecting cars, coins, or antiques in an attempt to fill an empty space within.

Despite all of our technological advances, despite the exploration of space, in the future our age will also be known for its preoccupation with eating—or *not* eating. Think of the ads on TV concerned with diet products and diet programs. Think about our nation's obsession with thinness. Check out the newspaper and yellow pages for restaurant ads and for fast-food specials. And what about concerns about low-cholesterol foods, oat bran, diet soda, and red meat?

As a nation we hunger for intimacy, we are starved for supportive relationships. We will probably eat our way into the twenty-first century and achieve nationwide obesity while starving spiritually.

Bread and Economics

The discovery of wheat in Europe and maize in the Americas—both about 10,000 years ago—changed the way humans lived. The invention of bread and tortillas allowed early humans to stop wandering day after day with the hunt and to settle down on the farm or in the village.

Imagine the first baker: someone ground seeds into flour, added some water to make a thick paste, and then perhaps wrapped the dough around a stick and cooked it over a fire. Voila!—the first flat bread, or thin bread. But what about fermentation and raised bread? Did that baker leave a floury mush too long in the sun? Or did someone actually set out to invent raised bread?

I grew up during the transition from home-baked bread to store-bought bread. The latter was a sign of the middle class and economic well-being. We referred to the so-called vitamin-enriched stuff as "air bread," since sandwiches from it inevitably got squashed down to paper-thin, doughy slices in lunch boxes. Nevertheless, I was conditioned to feel sorry for a friend of mine, Wayne Larson, whose mother baked bread; he was forced to eat *homemade* bread and peanut butter. Couldn't the Larsons afford store-bought bread?

Economics and class status affect food choices. Greeks and Romans, for example, distinguished between white bread and dark bread. The dark, coarse bread, called *panis sordidus* (paltry bread) by the Romans, was associated with peasant life; white bread meant status. Their legacy means that today large numbers of children never taste real whole-wheat or rye bread.

In the 1950s and 1960s it was possible to trace the growth of the middle class in Mexico with the substitution of Pan Bimbo for their wonderful rolls (*bolillos*) and fresh tortillas; Pan Bimbo, the same tasteless white bread we had grown up with in the Midwest, was introduced to Mexico by an American company, along with Aunt Jemima pancakes. I have a strong memory from 1968 of Mexican women in Tlaquepaque, Jalisco, slapping tortillas into shape and cooking them on a hot flat stone. We bought them warm for dinner; butter melted on them, and they melted in our mouths—better than any cake or cookies.

Food

Windmill cookies at the Hollenbergs',
Fried rice and chop suey at the Tiens',
Tortillas at the Gutierrezes',
Bagels, lox, and cream cheese at my house.
Steak at the Ohlbaums' (they have lots of money).
One meat, one starch, two vegetables, and milk at
    the Shermans' (they're an athletic family).
I eat natural food,
Drug addicts and alcoholics eat almost no food,
Rich people eat expensive food,
Poor people eat lots of starches.

Eat over other peoples' houses sometime.
You will learn . . .
    Families are what they eat.

—Dan S./HS

Food, Family, and Community

When my children were old enough to go to friends' houses for meals, they were surprised to learn that some families do not eat together, and if they do eat together many do not talk during the meal. In these families, the ingestion of food has been reduced to an act of physical sustenance. A truly poignant image is the old man or woman eating alone at a corner table in some crowded urban cafeteria.

On the home front, food equals power. For past generations—and present—it was one of the most important sources of power for women, who were disenfranchised in many other areas of life. Loving one's mom meant eating her meals, especially her holiday meals. Certain mothers are stereotyped as equating matzoh balls or spaghetti with nurturing, but obviously the pattern stretches across all racial and ethnic lines. The parents of one of my students made her eat in the kitchen until she was fourteen years old. Her manners were not suitable for eating in the dining room with her parents. What kinds of lessons might she have learned from this experience?

The Book of Mark in the New Testament relates the story of a famous meal involving the feeding of five thousand people. After three days of preaching, Jesus wanted to feed his listeners. He took seven loaves of bread and a few fish provided by his disciples and fed the whole group, with seven baskets of leftovers. A teacher friend of mine asked a student how this was possible. The student explained: when it was time for lunch, everyone was kind of cagey, looking around at first. Then when Jesus shared all that he had with the crowd, all the others reached into their robes and pulled out the sandwiches they had brought with them, and with open hearts shared food with their group. Everyone had plenty, even those who had forgotten to bring anything. There is always plenty of food if people will share what they have.

Sharing personal experiences during mealtimes is as important as filling the belly. Family histories are built from these conversations; lives are woven together into a spiritual community. For my own family, this is reason enough for giving thanks before actually eating.

The communal meal has long symbolized both a social bond and a religious bond between those who eat together. It was an ancient Semitic law of hospitality that the host who sat down to eat with his guest had to provide safety for his guest, even if previously they had been enemies. A saying which symbolized this bond was "There is salt between us" (Smith, 269ff.).

Culture Shock

They look at me funny,
Whisper a little.
Make scowls and groans
And think they'll be sick.

Suddenly I,
Who had been oblivious
Smashing my cornbread
Into my beans,
Look up at the
Astonished faces.
—What are you doing?—
They implore in horror.
—Why this is the only way
to eat pinto beans, wish I
had onions—
And lose ten friends in a sentence.

But how could they understand, they
Who have never eaten
Cornbread in buttermilk,
Blackeyed peas
On New Year's eve, or
Southern fried potatoes
On a humid summer evening?

—Jill O./HS

Bread, Wine, and Religion

Food and religion are closely connected. The most important early deities, after the creators, were the goddesses of agriculture and the gods of weather. In ancient Greece, Zeus was originally a god of lightning and rain, and Demeter was the goddess of vegetation; her counterpart in Roman mythology was Ceres, from whom we get *cereal*.

The word *bread* (meaning also food in general) appears 322 times in the Bible, a repetition reflecting concern with spiritual as well as physical survival. Undoubtedly, the first religious ceremonies had the sacred feast as a central activity. What was originally a biological need met by chomping on an animal's thigh bone became eating the god's thigh, serving a psychological need for communion with other humans and the gods. (Incidentally, the word *sacred* is linked to the Latin *sacrum*, which was the sacred bone of an animal used in sacrifices.)

Food took on a religious role through a simple metaphor: to ingest a particular substance is to incorporate the spiritual properties of that substance into one's being; an animal sacred to a particular deity was eaten by worshippers as an act of ingesting the powers and wisdom of that god. In Greece the bull, sacred to Poseidon, was sacrificed and eaten in Poseidon's honor with the hope of communing with the god and gaining his power. Certain kinds of cannibalism also seem to originate with this basic idea: to eat a small portion of a dead warrior was to ingest his valor, bravery, or strength.

Bread and wine were favored by early Christians for rites of communion. Worshippers of Osiris, Adonis, and Dionysus also used bread and wine (see Walker). Wine symbolizes the liquid of life, the blood of life. Bread is more complex and is analogous to various facets of a human being: flour and water correspond to flesh and blood; yeast is the promoter of growth; salt adds character. (Do you know any flat characters? Any bland or salty characters?) The fire which transforms dough into bread is equivalent to the pain and suffering which transform an undifferentiated consciousness into a person of character.

Bread figures were used as magical charms in many cultures. The Aztecs in Mesoamerica shaped bread dough into images of their favorite deity, Huitzilopochtli. At the end of his feast day, the celebrants broke the dough images into pieces and ate them as an act of communion with the god. Fray Duran describes this act:

> The people claimed that they had eaten the flesh and bones of the gods, though they were unworthy. Those who had sick ones at home begged for a piece and carried it away with reverence and

veneration. All those who received the communion were obliged to give tithes of the same seed which had formed the dough of the flesh and bones of the god. (95)

In Mexico, the Day of the Dead is still celebrated with a procession to the cemetery and a picnic among the gravestones with bread formed into a skull and crossbones. It is a widespread belief that at least once during the year the dead have access to the living, are able to pass over to this side and dine with the living. Places are set for the dead souls at the table, and food and drink are provided (Frazer, 398ff.).

Communion

"Take, eat this in remembrance of me."
But meals go by. No time for breakfast
Study at lunch
Supper on the run.

"Your body is a temple."
Why feed it that?
Candy Bars, Big Macs,
Greasy french fries soak their wrapper
With day-old oil.
Plaster ice cream with artificial strawberries.

Whatever happened to Grandma's
Roastbeef dinners with real mashed potatoes
And home-made gravy?
Whatever happened to real family get-togethers?

—Becky T./HS

Eating in New Mexico

Eat, hijita, eat. You don't have hungry?
No tienes hambre? Tortillas, sopaipillas, green
chile y frijoles, posole, biscochitos, empanadas.
Grandma Alcaria pushed us to eat, always. It was
an insult to refuse her cooking. And if you did,
you were probably sick. Holiday tables filled up,
as she waddled back & forth with her creations.
There was little conversation, we were busy eating.
Although we pushed food in with a certain amount
of desperation, forks glided politely to our mouths.
We watched Grampa Tomas lightly dab the sweat from
his forehead, beads forming from eating hot red chile.

All the men ate first, like Adolph, whose soft, full
lips covered by a black moustache could have belonged
to Emiliano Zapata. Those thick lips sucked off the
whole jalapeno, hot & forbidden, as he wiped his mouth
and reached for a tall glass of agua. Uncle Phil
cleverly balanced a beer or a glass of wine in one hand,
scooped chile and beans into his mouth with a folded
piece of tortilla, and still managed to converse
brilliantly with everyone around him.

Wives and daughters joined the table only after the
men claimed a seat, only if there was room enough.
Grandma Alcaria, after the job was complete, quieres
mas cafe?, after she added another stick of butter,
replenished the tortilla stack, brought Adolfo another
glass of water, would find the smallest plate, serve
one scoop of beans and chile from the kitchen pots,
and sit down at the kitchen table, alone.
Do you want to eat in the dining room?
No, it's okay. Eat, hijita, eat.

—Catherine B./C

Ceremony and Celebration

Traditionally, people have thought of time in terms of cycles, which
periodically, rhythmically renew themselves: the turn of the seasons,
the annual journey of the sun north and then back south, periods of
rain and drought. Cycles of the moon, corresponding to the monthly
cycles of women, marked off periods of the earth's fertility and indicated
exact times for plowing, sowing, and harvesting.

The basis for ritual corresponds to the need to set aside particular
holidays during which the energy of the community can be focused
on the passageway, the movement across the threshold, from the old
to the new. The annual cycles in nature—from planting to harvest—are
paralleled by the stages of human life: birth, puberty, marriage, and
death. The need for holidays or festivals led to the development of a
religious calendar and the creation of literature.

From earliest times, the human imagination has cast seasonal crises
and their resolutions in dramatic terms: as conflicts between the forces
of light and dark, spring and winter, sky and earth. Each morning the
sun defeats the forces of night, rises to a noonday triumph, and slowly
recedes toward defeat at sunset. Annually, the infant New Year must
defeat the aging Year-King, whose reign is finished on December 31.
Each spring vegetation must force its way out of the underworld
dungeon in order to sprout and mature. For centuries the natural cycles

provided a model for social organization, as groups or clans within a society took on various roles in the seasonal dramas. Each year the world was reborn; people could leave behind the mistakes of the past year and begin again.

Holidays, then, are periods of renewal, and also periods of release. A kind of rhythm in nature flows between death and life, scarcity and abundance, work and play, drought and flood. At one extreme, humans need to make plans, to conserve seed for the next planting, to store surplus food for the winter—to be *practical*. But the other side to the natural rhythm, associated with harvest, with plentitude or abundance, is something in the human spirit that wants to *let go* and to celebrate nature's goodness. We find this exuberant spirit in the colors of autumn, the songs of birds, the varieties of flowers, the leaping of dolphins, and the human desire to sing, parade, and dance when hearts are full of joy.

Poetry expresses the seasons of the heart; it is the essential language of ceremony.

Old Indians dance
Pressing their feet into earth
Making love each step.

          —Barbara B./C

The Birthday Party

Tonight I am handed
a bigger piece of cake
than usual, and a fork

I remember as a child.
A balloon inscribed
"FORTY" pops up,
and is lightly
batted about the room.
The punch has a jocular

ring. The cake and fork
are still on my lap.
It's time, they say,

to unwrap the present.
Now the double-headed
candle is trotted out.

Here is the card from
the humor section. Hey,
a bottle of prune wine.

And why not? The year
passes; the dog barks.
The moon grins

in the twigs of an elm.
The sound is my fork hitting the plate.

— Jon K./C

The One Voice

sometimes in the great circle
of the spring pow wow
all the people will sing together
a soft chorus of beauty
a deep song of power
this is the one voice of the people
all the earth pauses to hear
it says that the people
will never leave the earth
each person is one voice in the song
the song binds the people together
it is many lives becoming one life

like the geese on their journey
like the winds in the storm
like the night speaking of the coyotes
like the summer singing of the insects
and the spring voices of the frogs
it is a great magic of the earth
which is all things singing together
saying we are here we are one
saying life is good life is eternal
saying beauty saying love

— Norman H. Russell

Classroom Activities

Discussion Questions

1. How has TV affected the family meal? A student complained about his mother who allowed him to eat supper in front of the TV: they stopped communicating.

2. How have fast-food places affected eating? Imagine a fast-food place of the future. When space flight was still new, it was predicted that soon people would be eating their meals out of tubes just like the astronauts. Was this a good idea? How would you simplify eating?

3. I once brought several small loaves of bread and a jar of honey to a writing class as a way of working with metaphors and celebration: "Bread is like poetry," "Poetry is like bread," "Honey is a food of the gods." When is food more than food?

4. Discuss the role of festival in our country—or the lack of it. Make a list of the festivals in your area. What takes place at these events? Do people have fun? Is the United States better at working than at playing? How does your family celebrate? Do you know of a religion or church group that knows how to celebrate? What do they do?

5. Some places in the world still practice true hospitality, where strangers in town are welcomed into peoples' homes and given a meal and a place to rest. Our family experienced this in Mexico and also in Greece. Has this happened to you?

6. The word *obese* comes from the Latin *obedere*, "to devour." Find a comfortable seat in an airline terminal or bus depot: observe the people there. Is America becoming obese? Check out our leaders in Washington. We have a slang expression, "fat cat," meaning the well-to-do banker or politician. Where do you think "fat cat" came from?

Writing Suggestions

1. Write about a holiday meal: it might be a single remembered meal, or an imaginative blend of several. Is there a single place where the relatives gather for the holidays? Who cooked what? Include bits of conversation. Who came? Were there humorous or sad incidents?

2. Bring to class sample menus from several restaurants; compare them. Create a favorite menu; make it so vivid the reader's mouth waters. Describe smells, tastes, sounds. You might repeat the phrase "My favorite food is. . . ."

3. A variation on the "favorite meal" theme is the absurd, crazy meal with strange food combinations: chocolate grasshoppers on squash ice cream. Or a disgusting menu fit for your worst enemy: toad eggs with hair sauce.

4. The Fruit and Vegetable Game: each student has a fruit or vegetable (the same as other students or different). The object of the game is for each student to closely examine the fruit or vegetable, noting its particular characteristics, and then to

introduce it to the rest of the class. Finally, students are to write poems about the fruit or vegetable:

An artist painting a lemon
must take a risk and splash
the vibrancy of yellow on the canvas.
The artist must accept the lemon
not for its inner bitterness
but for its exterior gaiety.

—Kelly W./HS

References

Duran, Fray Diego. 1971. *"Book of the Gods and Rites" and "The Ancient Calendar."* Translated and edited by Fernando Horcasitas and Doris Heyden. Norman, Okla.: University of Oklahoma Press.

Frazer, Sir James. 1964. *The New Golden Bough.* Edited by T. H. Gaster. New York: New American Library.

Russell, Norman H. 1980. *Indian Thoughts: My Journey.* Marvin, S.D.: Blue Cloud Quarterly (vol. 26, no. 2).

Smith, W. Robertson. 1972 [1889]. *The Religion of the Semites: The Fundamental Institutions.* New York: Schocken Books.

Walker, Barbara G. 1988. *The Woman's Dictionary of Symbols and Sacred Objects.* San Francisco: Harper & Row.

9 Work

The dominant image for work since the industrial revolution of the nine-teenth century has been the machine. Say this word and wheels begin to spin in the head: visions of steamboats on the Mississippi, automobile factories in Detroit, enormous turbines inside Hoover Dam, and kitchens filled with appliances. City dwellers—that is, most of us—are surrounded by machines, the steady hum and din from morning to night.

The machine is a powerful image, and an even more powerful metaphor. Seventeenth-century science gave birth to a mechanistic view of nature. Eighteenth-century deists compared the cosmos to the fine workings of a clock. Rationalists of the nineteenth and twentieth centuries believed that the machine model could be applied to humans as well as nature, in order to create the well-ordered society.

The myth of the modern world, the myth of progress, proclaims that technology—the father of machines—has brought us easier, healthier, safer, and happier lives than the lives led by earlier generations. Progress, however, is accompanied by the assembly line, planned obsolescence, pollution, and stress.

Work in Ancient Israel and Greece

In the Bible, gardening is the first kind of "work": "The Lord God took the man and put him in the garden of Eden to till it and keep it" (Genesis 2:15). Since this was before the Fall, we can assume that this work was not arduous, but rather some kind of light pruning and plucking. One of the universal characteristics of the primeval garden or paradise is an abundance of food, which leaves leisure time for frolicking and feasting.

Adam and Eve, however, ate of the apple, learned how to distinguish good from evil, and were kicked out of Eden. The Hebrew God, Yahweh, radically changed the nature of work by chastising Adam and cursing the ground:

119

Accursed be the soil because of you.
With suffering shall you get your food from it
every day of your life.
It shall yield you brambles and thistles,
and you shall eat wild plants.
With sweat on your brow
shall you eat your bread,
until you return to the soil,
as you were taken from it.
For dust you are
and to dust you shall return.

(Genesis 3:17–19, *Jerusalem Bible*)

Sweat. The sweat of one's brow. *Sweat* is a vivid word. Sweat is the partner of drudgery, work that is our adversary. Physical sweat bursts from our pores in the hot sun while plowing the field; mental sweat comes from pressure in the office. From this word, we also get *sweat-box*, *sweatshop*, and *sweat suit*. On the positive side, though, sweat is seen by some as a part of a purification process, as in the Native American sweat lodge ceremony. And Yahweh himself rewarded honest toil with abundant harvests and prosperity.

Ancient Greece had its own version of the fall into work. The poet Hesiod (8th century B.C.) describes the five ages of humankind: the first, very much like Eden, was the Golden Age, when humans "lived with happy hearts, untouched by work or sorrow" (*Hesiod*, 62). But with each successive age—the Silver, the Bronze, and the Age of Heroes—conditions grew worse, until history arrived at the present age, the Iron Age:

This is the race of iron. Now, by day,
Men work and grieve unceasingly; by night,
They waste away and die. The gods will give
Harsh burdens, but will mingle in some good;
Zeus will destroy this race of mortal men,
When babies shall be born with greying hair.

(*Hesiod*, 64)

One of the most popular heroes of ancient Greece was Heracles (or Hercules), the prototype for our own present-day Mr. Clean. He went around the countryside performing gigantic, overwhelming jobs, cleaning out stables, purifying water systems, destroying putrid, diseased monsters.

Is work a curse or a blessing? The messages from the ancient world are mixed. The classical Greek male attended to the responsibilities of citizenship and friendship; manual labor and making money were left to the lower classes and slaves. The dominant males of northern Europe, however, were forced to greater exertions by the harshness of the climate. They were suspicious of tropical regions where fruits and vegetables were abundant, and where the natives spent as much time singing and dancing as sweating in the fields—or so it seemed. After all, we humans were kicked out of the garden.

Work in America: Jobs and the Working Blues

Slaves were forced to come to this country, but millions of immigrants chose to come, seeking a chance to work. Their vision of the New Eden was not a place for lounging around and picking fruit, but a virgin continent and the opportunity to begin anew with land, job, house, and family. Walt Whitman's poetry is filled with the excitement and promise of America: the energy of the frontier, the variety of peoples, backgrounds, landscapes, jobs, dreams. His writing celebrates democracy. Listen to his litany of work from "A Song for Occupations":

> House-building, measuring, sawing the boards,
> Blacksmithing, glass-blowing, nail-making, coopering, tin-roofing,
>   shingle-dressing
> Ship-joining, dock-building, fish-curing, flagging of sidewalks by
>   flaggers,
> The pump, the pile-driver, the great derrick, the coal-kiln and
>   brick-kiln,
> Coal-mines and all that is down there, the lamps in the darkness,
>   echoes, songs, what meditations, what vast native thoughts
>   looking through smutch'd faces,
> Iron-works, forge-fires in the mountains or by river-banks, men
>   around feeling the melt with huge crowbars, lumps of ore,
>   the due combining of ore, limestone, coal, . . .

A later poet in the Whitman tradition is Carl Sandburg. His famous poem "Chicago" is a tribute to the burly, energetic workman and to a vital city. It is a city which has two faces, however:

> They tell me you are wicked and I believe them, for I have
>   seen your painted women under the gas lamps luring the
>   farm boys.
> And they tell me you are crooked and I answer: Yes, it is true
>   I have seen the gunman kill and go free to kill again.
> And they tell me you are brutal and my reply is: On the faces
>   of women and children I have seen the marks of wanton
>   hunger.
> And having answered so I turn once more to those who sneer
>   at this my city, and I give them back the sneer and say to
>   them:

> Come and show me another city with lifted head singing so
>   proud to be alive and coarse and strong and cunning.
> Flinging magnetic curses amid the toil of piling job on job,
>   here is a tall bold slugger set vivid against the little soft
>   cities; . . .

Sandburg thought that a poet should attend to real life; Chicago certainly was real.

For countless immigrants, the curse of the old world followed them into the new: children laboring in factories; women hunched over sewing machines in sweatshops; danger and hardship in coal mines and steel mills; stoop labor in lettuce and tomato fields. For large segments of the population, work was not heroic, but a grind. Lives were worn down and worn out by labor.

What kept people at work, what kept their noses to the grindstone? The obvious answer is that they worked in order to eat, but the new American Eden also held out the promise of a larger, spiritual reward. Rooted in New England, puritanism spread throughout the American frontier, reinforcing the principles of industry and thrift by coloring them with religious duty and dreams of salvation.

In addition to the avenues of preaching and teaching, the folk wisdom of work was passed down through sayings, folktales, and proverbs:

> A stitch in time saves nine.

> A bird in the hand is worth two in the bush.

America, of course, had its own proverb maker in Benjamin Franklin. In *Poor Richard's Almanack* are sayings like the following:

> God helps them who help themselves.

> Early to bed and early to rise. Makes a man
> healthy, wealthy, and wise.

> Little strokes fell great oaks.

Puritanism, however, dampened the individual life with drab, sober grays, as if the burdens of life were to be accepted without humor, without the leaven of art and drama, poetry and dance. The Puritan was suspicious of carnal joys, suspicious of play in any form. However, it is not clear that God meant work to be an end in itself. Do we live to work or work to live?

America taught the work ethic very effectively; most of us growing up in this country ingested the message at the dinner table and made life plans accordingly. I grew up believing that art, especially poetry, was not legitimate work—a Puritan legacy in the Midwest. For many, the Puritan pendulum swung too far in one direction. Psychology speaks about "workaholics," men and women incapable of play, who actually work on their days off. We hear about men who retire from a lifetime of work and drop dead shortly thereafter.

Unfortunately, contemporary work has not escaped the drudgery usually associated with blue-collar factory jobs. According to Studs Terkel, both blue-collar and white-collar workers can sing the work-aday blues:

> The blue-collar blues is no more bitterly sung than the white-collar moan. "I'm a machine," says the spot-welder. "I'm caged," says the bank teller, and echoes the hotel clerk. "I'm a mule," says the steelworker. "A monkey can do what I do," says the receptionist. "I'm less than a farm implement," says the migrant worker. "I'm an object," says the high-fashion model. Blue collar and white call upon the identical phrase: "I'm a robot." (xiv)

I Don't Believe in Cremation

Have you heard?
This is the Promised Land
Fields of grain
And acid rain
But it's all that we have

A thousand colors
And a thousand kingdoms
Speak a thousand tongues
   Who listens
   Who understands?
The battle's under a finger
Under a second?
Where were we
Ten thousand years before?
Where will we be
Ten years from now?

      —Jon W./C

Tired Bakery

Went to the tired bakery today
and perused muffins without charm,
dilapidated cream puffs
colorless icings
shingle cookies
petrifying behind display cases
marked graphically—do not touch

age had crept into the goodies
sweet enthusiasm had ceased.

The over-worn cashier
looked as listless
as all the wares
I interrupted her stare
and thought I could invert
her gloomy day with a smile
The corners of her mouth winced
as if her face would break
but then the smile suddenly retreated
and she punched her button
the register rang
    no sale.

—J. T. F./C

In the coal mining towns of Colorado there was always a steam
whistle. It would sound once in the morning to let the men know
it was time to start work. It sounded once at noon for lunch and
once in the evening at quitting time. But whenever the whistle blew
three times, it meant someone had been killed in the mine. My
father remembered all the children being released from school when
the whistle sounded three times. They would all run to the main
opening of the mine to see if it was their father or brother who had
been killed.

—Emilio T./C

Working Images for the Young Writer

The ant. Symbolic of strength in numbers, the model of industry and
cooperation. A challenge to the Darwinian principle that competition
is the only key to survival within a single species.

The bee. "Busy as a bee." The model of hierarchy, a class society. The
drone is the male honeybee whose sole purpose is to fertilize the queen
bee. He does no work and is the rich playboy in bee society. The workers
are sterile or sexually imperfect female bees. And the queen bee is at
the top of the hierarchy; all that wonderful sweetness is due to a
matriarchy.

The English Romantic poet John Keats said that he would rather be
the flower than the bee:

> Now it is more noble to sit like Jove than to fly like Mercury—let
> us not therefore go hurrying about and collecting honey, bee-like
> buzzing here and there impatiently from a knowledge of what is
> to be aimed at; but let us open our leaves like a flower and be passive

and receptive—budding patiently under the eye of Apollo and taking hints from every noble insect that favors us with a visit—sap
will be given us for meat and dew for drink. (124)

Conspicuous consumption. This image brings to mind consumers, the
consuming public, the consumer index of the economy, *The Consumer's
Guide,* and *Consumer Weekly.* The word *consume* comes from the Latin
consumere, to "use up, eat, waste."

Consumption is the metaphor for modern life; to sketch or picture
it, you must begin with a baby's mouth filled with pablum or a lion
consuming the wildebeest. Then enlarge the image until it fills the
whole page, an empty closet, a garage, Carlsbad Caverns, a black hole.
The American dream has turned into cars, stereos, TVs, VCRs,
microwave ovens, jogging outfits, and computers. In our society, consumption is not only healthy but patriotic.

Division of labor. In 1776 Adam Smith pointed out in his *Wealth of
Nations* that economic production received its biggest boost from the
division of labor. His famous example was the production of pins. A
single workman performing all of the steps for manufacturing a pin
might actually produce a handful in a day; in contrast, a factory that
Smith had visited divided the process into eighteen steps performed
by ten different specialized workers, and together they produced more
than forty-eight thousand pins per day.

By the time Henry Ford used the division-of-labor model to build
a factory for his Model-T Fords, the number of operations was not
eighteen, but 7,882 specialized jobs. It is difficult to have pride in the
finished product—pride in your work—if you are only responsible for
a small step in the total production.

Housework. Is housework real work? Will men do it? Some women
work at a job outside the home and then do most of the housework
and cooking besides; in fact, one study found that "employed women
with children do only about two hours less domestic labor per day than
do non-employed women with children" (Kotz, 60).

Junk. Obsolescence and waste have created a crisis in junk: car
graveyards and garbage dumps. Storage sheds and houses and tourist
shops overflow with junk.

In the 1960s a major eastern city offered to pick up people's junk for
free, just to relieve citizens of worthless items. Everyone was amazed
at the amount of stuff that ended up on the curb: old washing machines,
dryers, TVs, tires, refrigerators, and so forth. And just ahead of the city
collectors were people in pickup trucks, even in Cadillacs, taking
advantage of the free junk.

In 1976 Thomas G. Pattinson decided that there was a market in actual junk; he put together a cardboard box containing a caved-in ping pong ball, a balloon with a hole in it, half of a wooden clothespin, a twisted bobby pin, an empty coffee jar, and other items. Stores in Dallas, Chicago, New York, and other major cities gave him big orders. Nieman-Marcus carried his line in their gift catalogue.

Machines. Most of us grew up with machines, so this image is easy to visualize, and the concept of *mechanism* is relatively easy to understand. The machine model—connoting order, efficiency, production, and management—can be readily applied to a wide variety of situations.

If nature runs like a machine (as was once widely thought), why shouldn't society be run the same way? Why shouldn't schools be run according to production models? Aren't families, after all, simply miniature factories with varying inputs and outputs according to age and size?

The great danger of a handy metaphor like the machine is that complex activities can too easily be reduced to simplistic, mechanical explanations. In other words, the danger is reductionism: love is reduced to bodily chemistry; illiteracy is reduced to school budgets; world peace and harmony between nations are reduced to questions of technology and stockpiles of armaments. A hideous example is the reduction of human beings to objects during the Holocaust: for example, a number of Nazi executives treated the bodies of dead Jews in the death camps as mechanical problems involving transportation and cremation (see Shirer, 1265ff.).

Obsolescence. If products can become obsolete, why not people? This question is very relevant today:

> Perhaps it is this specter that most haunts working men and women: the planned obsolescence of people that is of a piece with the planned obsolescence of the things they make. Or sell. It is perhaps this fear of no longer being needed in a world of needless things that most clearly spells out the unnaturalness, the surreality of much that is called work today. (Terkel, xxii)

Gardening: An Alternative Metaphor

Several characteristics of gardening make it attractive: it involves nurturing and growing in a healthy environment; you can see the end product and use it. Ralph Waldo Emerson concluded a definition of success with the following: "To leave the world a bit better whether by a healthy child, a garden patch or a redeemed social condition; to know that even one life has breathed easier because you have lived." Gardening can be a metaphor for teaching, nursing, counseling, writing, or building—to name the more obvious.

During the 1960s, Helen and Scott Nearing (authors of *Living the Good Life: How to Live Sanely and Simply*) became models for the back-to-the-earth movement. The Nearings had retreated from an urban academic life to the Vermont woods, where they built their own dwellings and grew their own food.

Wendell Berry maintains that today large numbers of people have found alternatives to the rat race:

> They are the home gardeners, the homesteaders, the city people who have returned to farming, the people of all kinds who have learned to do pleasing and necessary work with their hands, the people who have undertaken to raise their own children. They have willingly given up considerable amounts of convenience—and considerable amounts of control, too—and have made their lives more risky and difficult than before.
>
> Why? For satisfaction, I think. And where does satisfaction come from? I think it comes from contact with the materials and lives of this world, from the mutual dependence of creatures upon one another, from fellow feeling. (62–63)

I wish I were not so organized,
the dustballs under my bed
arranged by size and color.
Every letter sent to me by anyone
is alphabetized and cross-referenced
by first and last names.
The watering schedules of my houseplants
are on my personal computer.
My magazine subscriptions are renewed
two months before I receive a notice.
I winterize my car in July.
If the government were to hire me,
I would organize Third World nations
by color-coded tabs
in my Trapper Keeper Data Center.

—Callie B./HS

Garbage Can . . .

. . . An anthology of the American public
laid waste
You probably contain more volumes than
the Library of Congress

—Stephen C./HS

Set Me Free

I'm tired of being glue
the kind that sticks
holds things together
keeps the family whole
patches broken hearts
cooks the meals
I'm tired of being
the insulation that muffles
the angry temper
of father toward son
sister toward sister
Cut the umbilical cord
open the gate
and set me free.

—Ingerid Clugston

Classroom Activities

Discussion Questions

1. What are your attitudes toward work? Sit down and quickly make a list of your associations with work. Do not try to make sense out of the items; just jot them down. Afterward you can reread the list and evaluate it. Discuss the associations with your classmates.

2. Within the last decade or so, the job market has opened up for women and various ethnic minorities. My mother grew up early in the twentieth century when there were generally two professional vocations open to women, teaching and nursing. What were the stereotypical jobs for blacks? For Chinese? For Irish? For Mexicans? Is there a historical basis for these stereotypes?

3. Are the adults you know happy in their work? A student talked about her father, who upholstered furniture: how he loved his work, the pride he felt in transforming an old beat-up couch into something new, beautiful, and useful. This pride and love for his work overflowed into other parts of his life, including family. Can unhappiness in a job affect other aspects of someone's life?

4. Do you remember the first occupation that appealed to you? My wife dearly wanted to be a truck driver on one of those big diesels with a double trailer. I wanted to be a bus driver. Why do some kids want to be firefighters or police officers?

5. No matter what the size of a town or city, we tend to divide it into zones according to the kinds of people living in each section. On big sheets of paper, draw a map of your city designating its sections. Where do the working-class people live? The doctors and lawyers? The retired people? Families with children? Ethnic minorities? Where do people work and where do they play?

Writing Suggestions

1. Write about the ideal job for you, whether it is something you might be able to do now or at some time in the future. Writing stems include "When I grow up..." and "I plan to be...."

2. A short formula poem can be written like this:

   Name: Bob Disco
   Job: a gas jockey
   Looks: has fuzz on his lip
   Action: shows girls how to jump-start a car

3. Suppose a family from outer space came to visit you and your hometown and you were their guide. To whom would you introduce them? Where would you take them for lunch? For recreation?

4. Write some proverbs in the style of Benjamin Franklin. For example, Elizabeth Fuller wrote her own "Poor Elizabeth's Almanac," and included proverbs such as "Step down an inch to help a friend and raise yourself a foot" and "Speak your mind but mind your speech."

5. Write fantastic, crazy proverbs, like "A car in the garage is worth two in the ditch," "Too many chilies spoil the taco," or "A joke in time is worth a dime."

6. Design a bumper sticker for your town.

7. Write a poem about how machines are becoming more human, and humans more mechanical. Write about humans from a machine's point of view.

References

Berry, Wendell. 1981. *The Gift of Good Land: Further Essays Cultural and Agricultural*. San Francisco: North Point Press. (Reprinted in *Utne Reader* [July/August 1988, pp. 62–63].)

Hesiod and Theognis. Translated by Dorothea Wender. 1981. New York: Penguin Books.

Keats, John. 1956. *The Selected Letters of John Keats,* edited by Lionel Trilling. Garden City, N.Y.: Doubleday and Company.

Kotz, David. *In These Times* (March 9, 1988). (Reprinted in *Utne Reader* [July/August 1988, p. 60].)

Shirer, William L. 1962. *The Rise and Fall of the Third Reich.* Greenwich, Conn.: Fawcett Publications.

Terkel, Studs. 1975. *Working.* New York: Avon Books.

Whitman, Walt. 1973. *Leaves of Grass.* Edited by Sculley Bradley and Harold W. Blodgett. New York: W. W. Norton & Co.

10 Nature and Balance

Imagine nature:

> A quiet pool of water
>
> Towering mountain peaks capped with snow
>
> Broad, rolling breakers along an ocean beach
>
> The dance of light across a shimmering desert
>
> A hawk floating effortlessly over the meadow
>
> The yellowed fangs of a grizzly bear, the smooth,
> glistening play of seals
>
> A lumbering elephant, a lusty goat, a cow chewing
> her cud, a pig wallowing in mud
>
> A sunset, a sunrise, a rainbow, lightning and thunder

Nature is the unlimited repository of images that send out ripples of feeling like a stone dropped into a pond. Nature and poetry, poetry and nature—they go together. Young poets, especially, associate the writing of poetry with special moments in nature: silver moonlight on the ocean, the awesome spires of the Grand Tetons, the dazzling display of autumn leaves in Vermont.

Words like *majesty, peace, timelessness, awe, beauty, sublimity, tranquility, joy,* and *fear* gain power through association with scenes from nature. Some of our oldest poems, such as hymns from ancient Egypt and psalms from the Old Testament, were inspired by nature's grandeur.

In nature are found both admirable and debased reflections of our own animal nature. In the passage from seed to harvest, from growth to decay, reside the inner meanings of time. With stone buildings and steel machines we can fool ourselves with the illusion of permanence and immortality, but not so with flora and fauna.

Various scenes inspire transcendence and flights of imagination, feelings for the magnificent and cosmic as well as for the microscopic and minuscule. We value nature for peace and quiet, for the opportunity it provides us to collect our wits, for spiritual revitalization.

131

Even so, with great callousness and arrogance humans have polluted and abused the natural world, eradicating some species of plants and animals and endangering others. It is imperative that we change our attitude and learn how to respect the natural world as a vast, inter-connected living web, so that all creatures on the planet earth may live in harmony:

> And hark! how blithe the throstle sings!
> He, too, is no mean preacher:
> Come forth into the light of things,
> Let Nature be your teacher.
>
> (William Wordsworth, "The Tables Turned")

Nature as a Mirror

Life in the woods provides a whole set of characters that mirror human nature: from the solitary wanderer and the communal chatterbox to the engaging thief with a black mask over his eyes. There are examples of strength and weakness, competition and cooperation, work and play, beauty and ugliness. Teachings are found in the grim cycle of life prey-ing on life, as well as in the scenarios of bravery and fortitude.

In "Wilderness," Carl Sandburg used creatures as metaphors to explore the shapes and desires of his psyche:

> There is a wolf in me ... fangs pointed for tearing gashes
> ... a red tongue for raw meat ... and the hot lapping
> of blood—I keep this wolf because the wilderness gave it
> to me and the wilderness will not let it go.
>
> . . . .
>
> There is a hog in me ... a snout and a belly... a machin-
> ery for eating and grunting ... a machinery for sleeping
> satisfied in the sun—I got this too from the wilderness and
> the wilderness will not let it go.
>
> There is a fish in me ... I know I came from salt-blue water-
> gates ... I scurried with shoals of herring ... I blew
> waterspouts with porpoises... before land was ... be-
> fore the water went down... before Noah... before
> the first chapter of Genesis.
>
> . . . .
>
> There is an eagle in me and a mockingbird... and the eagle
> flies among the Rocky Mountains of my dreams and fights
> among the Sierra crags of what I want ... and the
> mockingbird warbles in the early forenoon before the dew
> is gone, warbles in the underbrush of my Chattanoogas of
> hope, gushes over the blue Ozark foothills of my wishes
> —And I got the eagle and the mockingbird from the
> wilderness.

> O, I got a zoo, I got a menagerie, inside my ribs, under my
> bony head, under my red-valve heart—and I got some-
> thing else: it is a man-child heart and woman-child heart:
> it is a father and a mother and lover: it came from God-
> Knows-Where: it is going to God-Knows-Where—For I
> am the keeper of the zoo: I say yes and no: I sing and
> kill and work: I am a pal of the world: I came from the
> wilderness.

Nature can also be a threat. At the dinner table, children are warned about becoming pigs or eating like a bird. The nightmare side to this process is found in Franz Kafka's story "Metamorphosis," in which a young man awakens one morning to find he has changed into a cockroach. Is it possible that we might physically change into what we are becoming spiritually? Such is the stuff of fable and books like George Orwell's *Animal Farm*. Another example comes from Greek mythology: the goddess Artemis caught a young voyeur, Acteon, spying on her bath and changed him into a stag, his essential nature; then he was chased by his own hounds and killed.

The example of metamorphosis in nature provides additional lessons: the repulsive grub and the wondrous butterfly, the ugly duckling and the beautiful swan. In *Saint Francis*, the Greek writer Nikos Kazantzakis has Brother Leo describe his particular faith in transformation:

> I believe I'm a caterpillar buried deep down under the ground.
> The entire earth is above me, crushing me, and I begin to bore
> through the soil, making a passage to the surface so that I can
> penetrate the crust and issue into the light. It's hard work boring
> through the entire earth, but I'm able to be patient because I have
> a strong premonition that as soon as I do issue into the light I shall
> become a butterfly. (68)

Accordingly there is hope that the immature will mature, that the gawky teenager will change into the graceful adult.

Beyond all the metaphors and lessons from nature are those rarer times when we awaken to the full dimensions of the present moment and see perhaps a ponderosa pine or a mule deer not as something to use but simply in its own glory and mystery.

At the Zoo

Giraffe
who could ever
neck with you
and not refuse
your bulging eyes
heavy lids
and long eyelashes?

Ostrich
I've seen your feathers
lying on mahogany tables
collecting dust.
And to think
that I saw you
only yesterday
alive
pecking at particles
shuffling sand
hiding your head.

　　　　　　　　　　—Lorena G./C

　　　　　　　On Safari

The hunter returned
said he'd trapped all the worst ones

His private zoo, he said
now caged the most dangerous

Sometimes he believed it.

But other times
when he crept down to look

He found his zoo empty
bars bent, doors swung wide

They were loose
roaming free in his head again.

　　　　　　　　　　—Russell S./C

Being a tree
the wind rippling through your hair
birds clutching you
sap running down your spine
you're on top of the world

　　　　　　　　　　—Jennifer J./JH

　　　　　　　When It Rains . . .

the tiny droplets softly hitting my face
sweet smell of the oven's mud

sound of giants stomping around the earth
lightning cracking high above setting clouds on fire

I smell the cool dampness pitter-patter
on the tin roof

my insides feel like bursting out
like the blooming of a rose
Drink it up and GROW!

—students/JH

The Living Earth

Ancient peoples looked at nature differently than we do. For them everything in the world was alive, sacred, and sentient. Stones, trees, animals, and plants all responded to them, and they in turn tried to live in harmony with the powers of the natural world. A myth of the Okanagon (a subtribe of the Salish) describes this kind of living earth:

> Old-One, or Chief, made the earth out of a woman, and said she would be the mother of all the people. Thus the earth was once a human being, and she is alive yet; but she has been transformed, and we cannot see her in the same way we can see a person. Nevertheless, she has legs, arms, head, heart, flesh, bones, and blood.
> The soil is her flesh; the trees and vegetation are her hair; the rocks, her bones; and the wind is her breath. She lies spread out, and we live on her. She shivers and contracts when cold, and expands and perspires when hot. When she moves, we have an earthquake. Old-One, after transforming her, took some of her flesh and rolled it into balls, as people do with mud or clay. These he transformed into the beings of the ancient world. (Bierhorst, 55)

If we do not think of a story like this in terms of truth or falsity, we can appreciate how a series of metaphors can shape our attitudes toward the world: whether we treat the earth as a living thing deserving of our care and respect, or whether we simply exploit it. The above story of the earth-goddess reminds us that the earth is sacred.

Several mythologies contain stories about a time when animals and humans communicated, even spoke the same language. Peoples who were dependent on the beneficence of nature felt a closeness to nature. For example, Plains Indians, who lived off the buffalo, felt a sacred kinship with the buffalo and referred to them as "four-leggeds."

Dominion and the Death of Nature

The Hebraic tradition emphasized a distinction between man and the sovereignty of God; furthermore, the uniqueness of man made him distinct from all other creatures. The idea grew that animals were to serve man's needs.

Over the centuries, the original intimate relationship between humans and nature was ruptured. This momentous change in consciousness is recorded in legendary history as the death of Pan, the great god of all living things in the ancient world. The first-century writer Plutarch tells the story about a voyage being made to Italy. As the ship neared the Echinades Islands, a voice called to Thamus, an Egyptian pilot on board, saying that he should announce that Pan is dead when they were near Palodes:

> Under the circumstances Thamus made up his mind that if there should be a breeze, he would sail past and keep quiet, but with no wind and a smooth sea about the place, he would announce what he had heard. So, when he came opposite Palodes, and there was neither wind nor wave, Thamus, from the stern, looking toward the land, said the words as he had heard them: "Great Pan is dead." Even before he had finished, there was a great cry of lamentation, not of one person, but of many, mingled with exclamations of amazement. (Otto, ix)

Christian legend maintains that Pan died on the day that Jesus was crucified. In terms of religion, it meant that Greek religion, with its pantheon of gods and goddesses, was being replaced by Christianity. In terms of consciousness, Pan's death meant that nature was no longer sacred and would be treated in a different, secular way, which accounts for the "cry of lamentation" in the story. The old intimacy with nature was gradually replaced by rationalism and widespread monotheism.

From that time forward Europeans had mixed, contradictory feelings toward nature: some people felt a closeness, a relationship with nature—vestiges of the pre-Christian intimacy. An example is St. Francis of Assisi (1181?–1226), who experienced profound feelings of kinship with the natural world. Francis called the sun brother and the moon sister; he referred to animals in familial terms and talked with birds.

The opposite attitude is that nature exists to serve our purposes. Some historians see the root of this attitude in the Book of Genesis in the Bible, in which God gives man "dominion" over the earth, the fish, the birds, and the cattle. The concept of *dominion* was interpreted as enabling humans to control and govern what was believed to be a fallen, material world. In the post-Renaissance world, technology, with its tremendous power, became the sophisticated extension of this attitude of domination.

One excuse for taking land from the indigenous Americans in our nation's own history was that they were not putting the land to good use. They were not farming it extensively nor exploiting it in a systematic way; in other words, they were not dominating it. In the mid-nineteenth century, the Nez Percé leader Smohalla gave a famous speech refusing the terms of reservation life:

My young men shall never work. Men who work cannot dream, and wisdom comes in dreams.

You ask me to plow the ground. Shall I take a knife and tear my mother's breast? Then when I die she will not take me to her bosom to rest.

You ask me to dig for stone. Shall I dig under her skin for bones? Then when I die I cannot enter her body to be born again.

You ask me to cut grass and make hay and sell it, and be rich like white men. But how dare I cut off my mother's hair? (Astrov, 85)

Poets deal in images: what image do you have of the white man's treatment of nature? Exploiter? Conservationist? Does legal possession of a piece of land give one the right to waste the natural resources of that land?

The odd thing seems to be that the more people control and manipulate nature, the more alienated and lonely they become. Undoubtedly, there is a basic principle here concerning the balance between control and freedom in a vital relationship.

One summer in Arches National Monument in Utah, I met two boys, both about eight years old, who bragged about the number of lizards they had killed, some of them with a BB gun. I told these young hunters that lizards have a desire to live, like all living creatures. It was probably a futile reminder on my part, but I did wonder about the social environment that cultivates this spirit of arbitrary killing. I remembered shooting birds with my first BB gun, especially the English sparrows, thinking they were pests anyway, overpopulating the backyard.

One branch of this attitude could go back to a feeling of abundance about America: there was plenty, and more than plenty, of everything. The plentiful passenger pigeon, however, was slaughtered wholesale by sporting men in the nineteenth century, and has been extinct since 1914. Another branch is human arrogance and contempt for nonhuman creatures. A change of attitude is required.

Rabbit—that's me,
Me and my little ones.

There are six now,
A fox got the seventh one.

There was nothing
I could do,
Nothing
I would have done.

It's Nature's Law.
Some have to die
So others may live.

We don't change things
just accept them.
That's the way it is.

                    —Colleen J./HS

                Reptile Gardens

I am 8 years old in dry grass
around the water tower in July

I catch lizards and want to keep them
forever for a week until I forget

They are in ravines, beneath boards
in back yards, blinking their nostrils

wavering side to side, a sensuous rhythm
delicate as paper flowers in a reptile garden

Thousands of them in my bed, licking me
pink tongues on my chin and thighs

but stiff and skeletal
in the bottom of a coffee can
they are almost as good

                                    —Carl P./C

Out of Balance: Ecological Disaster

Human beings and industry have changed the face and body of Mother
Nature. Instead of using nature as an inspirational model for cleaning
up our cities, we have slowly polluted woods and lakes, reducing them
to areas of sickness that are consistent with dirty factories and run-down
neighborhoods.

Rachel Carson's *Silent Spring*, published in 1962, brought the word
ecology into modern consciousness. She began her book with a fable
about an ordinary town in the heartland of America where prosperity
culminates in the death of all vegetation, birds, and animals.

Although there is at present no single town like this, the fable is pro-
phetic since individual parts of the fable have happened somewhere,
and it is possible that in the future all the parts could come together
in a single place, resulting in a real silent spring. Carson's chapter titles
ring ominously: "Elixirs of Death," "And No Birds Sing," "Rivers of
Death," "Indiscriminately from the Skies." Since 1962 the dangers to
our environment have multiplied, and the all-too-familiar list of the
polluted and the pollutants sounds like a litany of doom:

Love Canal	Bhopal	Chernobyl
Three Mile Island	DDT	asbestos
vinyl chloride	acid rain	yellow rain
red tide	Agent Orange	CFCs and PCBs

To these, we could add the hundreds of species on the endangered list, America's contaminated drinking water, the destruction of the ozone layer, the greenhouse effect, communities threatened by hazardous waste dumps, and so on and so on.

Needed: A Change of Attitude

As a start, young writers need to take a good look at the underbelly of civilization, the price we pay for automobiles and insecticides. Despite repeated warnings about imbalances in nature and the threat of various kinds of pollution, despite indications that health and happiness are threatened by continued abuses of our natural environment, our society marches on, placing its faith in progress, trusting that some lifesaving technology is around the corner.

Since pollution involves everything—from recycling household waste to environmental controls on the state and national level—change means more than laws and compliance; change necessitates a change in our attitude toward nature. An excerpt from a speech by Chief Seattle in 1852 reflects an alternative, organic perspective:

> This we know. The earth does not belong to man, man belongs to the earth. This we know. All things are connected like the blood which unites one family. All things are connected. Whatever befalls the earth befalls the sons of earth. Man did not weave the web of life, he is merely a strand in it. Whatever he does to the web, he does to himself. (422)

This idea of a vast organic, interconnected system is not new; it is a primary theme in most mythologies around the world. A fundamental tenet of ecology is this organic web connecting all parts and creatures on the earth. Disturbances in ecological balance in one part of the world affect the balance in other parts of the world. The disappearance of the elephant in Africa is related to the brown smog hanging over Los Angeles in the mornings.

With the invention of the airplane, public attention increasingly turned away from the earth and was directed to the scientific investigation of the sky. The imagination of the whole world was captured by Russia's and the United States' exploration of space. Powerful voices in government and industry promoted projects involving the economic, technological, and military uses of rockets, satellites, and space vehicles. Space was the new frontier, and we entered a new age where we looked to the sky for answers.

In recent years, however, massive damage to the earth's ecosystem has awakened the consciousness of people throughout the world. I believe that writers in particular must make their voices heard in an ever-widening, more audible chorus.

John Steinbeck learned a marvelous new way to hunt bighorn sheep (*borrego*) in Baja California. After packing into the mountains, Steinbeck remained in camp talking with his rancher host while the Indian guides took a 30-30 carbine off to hunt. They eventually returned without a sheep, but with a pocketful of sheep droppings, which they shared with Steinbeck and the rancher. Steinbeck comments:

> They had taught us the best of all ways to go hunting, and we shall never use any other. We have, however, made one slight improve-ment on their method: we shall not take a gun, thereby obviating the last remote possibility of having the hunt cluttered up with game. . . . Often a man who is afraid must constantly demonstrate his courage and, in the case of the hunter, must keep a tangible record of his courage. For ourselves, we have had mounted in a small hardwood plaque one perfect borrego dropping. And where another man can say, There was an animal, and because I am greater than he, he is dead and I am alive, and there is his head to prove it, we can say, There was an animal, and for all we know there still is and here is proof of it. He was very healthy when we last heard of him. (166–67)

We must find the means of feeling at home on this planet, to find im-ages of reconciliation with nature. In "Song of Myself," Whitman uses ordinary grass to make extraordinary connections:

> A child said *What is the grass?* fetching it to me with full hands;
> How could I answer the child? I do not know what it is any
>   more than he.
>
> I guess it must be the flag of my disposition, out of hopeful green
>   stuff woven.
>
> Or I guess it is the handkerchief of the Lord,
> A scented gift and remembrancer designedly dropt,
> Bearing the owner's name someway in the corners, that we may
>   see and remark, and say *Whose?*
>
> Or I guess the grass is itself a child, the produced babe of the
>   vegetation.
>
> Or I guess it is a uniform hieroglyphic,
> And it means, Sprouting alike in broad zones and narrow zones,
> Growing among black folks as among white,

Kanuck, Tuckahoe, Congressman, Cuff, I give them the same, I
  receive them the same.
And now it seems to me the beautiful uncut hair of graves.

It remains to be seen whether poets—all artists, all creative people—in
our modern society will help transform the instruments of war and
pollution into aids to planetary healing and growth.

WASP

I'm glad to be a WASP:
(White American Succulent Potato)
Turgid cells of starch,
Vitamins B, C, G
and high-class protein.
I can look any other
Russet in the eye.

Not so,
my cousin, the yam,
who spills her
yellow guts for all
and leaves her cloying smile
on someone's dinner plate.
Syrup-popped skin, empty shell.

I'm the only blue-blood
in the garden
who shares a monument
with Sir Francis Drake.
It is so recorded
in our family history.

—Nancy M./C

Schizophrenic

I love you,
I hear you
In mountain streams
That only speak
So loudly
Here, away from people.
I see you,
In the Aspens
Standing tall and proud
And swaying in the wind.
I feel you
In the breeze
That disturbs the rotting leaves,
The dark, natural foundation.

The wind that
Is your soul, my brother,
And the wilderness
That is your life.

—Jill O./HS

So, you've never been to the ocean before.
Well, let me show you.
I'll take you where the tidepools are,
To the little one under the shadow of a rock,
Where the hermit crabs and starfish are.
I'll teach you
How to walk along the shore,
So only the edges of your rolled-up jeans
Get wet.
I'll show you
How to dive into a wave,
How to know when to come up
The right way to ride a wave back
Into shore.
I'll teach you
The exact time to dig for sandcrabs,
As the wave goes out,
Just before it is completely gone.
I'll take you,
In your bare, sandy feet and wet, rolled-up jeans,
To a restaurant,
Tiny and disreputable.
One that you would never go to
On your own.
But one that serves the best fish and chips
You ever tasted in your life.
We will get an ice-cream cone,
And walk along the beach,
Trying to eat it before
It melts.
I'll show you
When to watch the sun sink into the sea,
Even though
You won't be able to tell
Exactly when it does.
We will sit,
In the damp sand,
And watch the dark side of the ocean,
Calm and not as playful.
You feel the power more
At night.
You will have seen the ocean
The way it should be seen,
With someone.

—Caren L./HS

When I am weaving, spinning or making a basket I feel in touch with the maternal, female side of my nature. The tools I work with in these crafts are all of the earth—my loom is made of wood, as is my spinning wheel. In making a basket I use as my core material reeds or fibre made from the bark of trees. My tapestry comb is made of wood, as is my warping board. The fibres I work with are all natural wool from sheep, cotton from plants, flax, camel hair, mohair. The process of weaving is rhythmic; spinning is cyclical as the wheel turns round and round. The forms are circular, meditative; and participating in these processes puts me in touch with my femaleness and with the earth.

—Sue S./C

Classroom Activities

Discussion Questions

1. Learning how to read nature is fascinating. Look at a natural object, such as a leaf, as if it contained a coded message. What is the message?

2. How is a human like a tree? An egg? A stone? A tumbleweed? Compare your feelings to a lake, a pond, or a desert.

3. Imagine that you could talk to particular animals or birds: which ones would you talk to? Is there anything that we could learn from particular animals?

4. Early peoples used particular animals as symbols for their families or clans. Which animal would you choose as a totem for your family?

5. Some people believe that we should think of birds and animals as our brothers and sisters. Would thinking in these terms change our attitudes and actions toward the rest of creation?

6. Read Kafka's short story "Metamorphosis." If you were changed into a nonhuman thing, what would it be?

Writing Suggestions

1. You only have to look to find poems outside: behind the bark of a tree, under a leaf, inside a scrap of paper flying down the street. Find an object and write about it.

2. When we write about animals, we usually want to make them come alive, and that means using active verbs and strong adjectives. Rather than painting a still-life portrait of an animal, describe the animal in a dramatic situation.

3. Make a list of extinct animals and birds. Make a list of endangered species. Did you include humans in this last list? Are there similarities between the animals on the list and humans? Imagine that you are the last member of a particular species; write about it.

4. We can discover inner feelings by association. Animals are like mirrors held up to humans; with certain animals we find humor and a chance to laugh at ourselves (see Paul Simon's song "At the Zoo"). Write about animals that make good mirrors. Write about the bird or animal within you.

5. Can you empathize with birds or animals? John Keats writes about using his imagination to identify with a bird: "If a Sparrow come before my Window I take part in its existence and pick about the Gravel" (Keats, 101). What would it feel like to be a shark, an ostrich, a flamingo?

6. In 1970, Capitol records released *Songs of the Humpback Whale,* and in 1977, *Deep Voices: The Second Whale Record.* Do whales actually sing? These records make a convincing case for believing they do. Listen to one or both of the records. Imagine what the whales are singing and write about it. The following are student responses to the whale records:

    It is a cow having a calf.
    A call from the dead
    Like a possessed person
    It is sonar on a ship.
    Like your dog in slow motion, barking away in the night
    A 78 record on 33

7. Whales are thought to be very intelligent, as are dolphins. Has anyone communicated with a dolphin? (The scientist John Lilly has done some research in this area.) What would such a conversation be like?

8. Stand up and stretch out your arms; close your eyes and spread your fingers like antennas; imagine that you are making contact with vibrations given off by other living things. What does it feel like?

    This energy feels like . . .
    I'm hanging from a rope in the sky.
    Birds going through my fingers
    Your bones trying to push away your skin
    Fire snakes shooting up my spine

9. Poets need to stand up for the earth. The earth is a living thing that demands care and attention. Write a slogan for the earth. Write an entire advertising campaign for the earth.

References

Astrov, Margot, ed. 1962. *American Indian Prose and Poetry.* New York: Capricorn Books.

Bierhorst, John, ed. 1976. *The Red Swan: Myths and Tales of the American Indians.* New York: Farrar, Straus and Giroux.

Carson, Rachel. 1970 [1962]. *Silent Spring.* Greenwich, Conn.: Fawcett Publications, Inc.

Keats, John. 1956. *The Selected Letters of John Keats.* Edited by Lionel Trilling. Garden City, N.Y.: Doubleday & Company, Inc.

Kazantzakis, Nikos. 1962. *Saint Francis.* Translated from the Greek by P. A. Bien. New York: Simon and Schuster.

Otto, Walter. 1965. *Dionysus: Myth and Cult.* Bloomington, Ind.: Indiana University Press.

Seattle, Chief. *The Washington Historical Quarterly* 22, no. 4 (October 1931). The Washington University State Historical Society, Seattle, Washington. (Reprinted in *The Great Cosmic Mother.* Monica Sjöö and Barbara Mor. San Francisco: Harper & Row, Publishers, 1987.)

Steinbeck, John. 1952. *The Log from the Sea of Cortez.* New York: Random House.

Wordsworth, William. 1965. *Selected Poems and Prefaces.* Edited by Jack Stillinger. Boston: Houghton Mifflin.

11 Dreams, Reveries, Monsters, and UFOs

From the very beginning of human consciousness people must have wondered about the mysteries of dream life. Dreams seem so vivid and real, filled with the extremes of horror and happiness, the heroic and the mundane.

Even though one-third of our lives is spent in sleep, the vast majority of books are written about the daytime world. Modern society emphasizes external realities and invests millions of dollars in physical appearances, cosmetics, and fashion; it invests billions of dollars in the exploration of outer space. But a whole region within waits for exploration; and it is virtually free:

> We are such stuff
> As dreams are made of, and our little life
> Is rounded with a sleep.
>
> (William Shakespeare, *The Tempest*)

This inner world is a vast treasury of images and stories waiting to be discovered by the poet. Furthermore, dream language has essentially the same ingredients as poetic language: image, metaphor, and symbol.

Besides being a resource for poets and other artists, the exploration of dreams brings other benefits: knowledge of the deeper self and the possibility of using this knowledge for mental health. Despite our high technology, we do not fully appreciate the influence of dreams and nightmares on our waking behavior. Our interest in monsters and UFOs might be a projection of this surreal landscape.

In the United States, with our wealth and advanced technology, we have emphasized the external, material world, and have really neglected the interior, hidden dimension of the psyche. It could be argued that debilitating stress, broken relationships, and even substance abuse are the results of this neglect. The words of Thomas Merton convey the importance of coming to terms with this inner world:

What can we gain by sailing to the moon if we are not able to cross the abyss that separates us from ourselves? This is the most important of all voyages of discovery, and without it all the rest are not only useless but disastrous. (11–12)

Dreams as Visitations from the Gods

Probably the oldest recorded dreams in history can be found in the *Epic of Gilgamesh*, a work of literature popular in Mesopotamia before 2,000 B.C. Gilgamesh, the king of Uruk, reports one of his dreams to his mother:

> I was full of joy, the young heroes were round me and I walked through the night under the stars of the firmament, and one, a meteor of the stuff of Anu, fell down from heaven. I tried to lift it but it proved too heavy. All the people of Uruk came round to see it, the common people jostled and the nobles thronged to kiss its feet; and to me its attraction was like the love of woman. They helped me, I braced my forehead and I raised it with thongs and brought it to you. (Sandars, 64)

His mother interpreted the dream by telling him about the arrival of a comrade, Enkidu, who would have divine strength, be like a brother, and influence Gilgamesh's future.

The Mesopotamians took dreams very seriously, and thought that the events taking place in dreams were real or predictive of future reality. A dream about a god meant that the god had actually visited the person in the dream. All the major temples had special dream rooms where people could make contact with the divine will. The priests used dream books to aid in interpreting the worshipers' dreams, diagnosing sickness and prescribing cures.

From the time of Homer to the first century B.C., the most famous center of healing for the entire Mediterranean area was Epidauros in Greece. Patients spent the night in healing rooms where their dreams would be interpreted as pathways to cures. These rooms were also visited by a harmless house snake.

Snakes were believed to have the power of rebirth (because they shed their skin), and were messengers to the powers beneath the earth (since the underworld is associated with the cycle of growth and rebirth). The Greek Asclepius became the model physician. He carried a staff with entwined snakes, the *caduceus*. This symbol was inherited from Mesopotamia and later became the symbol for the medical profession

Figure 2. The caduceus,
or staff of Asclepius,
is an age-old symbol
of healing.

(Fig. 2). The wings of the caduceus indicate the sky, transcendence, and inspiration; the wand or staff is the *axis mundi*, the tree in the middle of the garden, the tree of life, the stable link between sky, earth, and underground. The twining serpents point to the necessary balance between light and dark, mind and body, male and female, to maintain or achieve health.

The significance of the caduceus and the snake imagery is apparent: the sick were being directed to explore the depths of their own unconscious as a medium of diagnosis. A reciprocal principle is at work here, a principle at the heart of holistic medicine today: if body and mind are the occasion for a sickness, then these same elements can be the occasion for the cure.

Twenty-eight occurrences of dreams are recorded in the Old Testament, thirteen of which are associated with a famous dreamer and dream interpreter, Joseph, who was made Pharaoh's right-hand man because of his dream skills (see Genesis 14).

A number of cultures have preserved the importance of dreams in their lives. For the Australian aborigines, the primordial time of creation, when the gods sorted out sky and earth, plants and animals, and all the rest, is called Dreamtime. It was a prehistorical time when mythological ancestors walked about the landscape establishing sacred objects and sacred places. The contemporary aborigine can participate in this sacred history through visiting these sacred places and dreaming there—an act which connects the dreamer to primordial reality and power.

One of the most unusual and fascinating groups to center their culture on dreaming is a jungle tribe in Malaya called the Senoi. They are extremely peaceful in behavior, and well respected by neighboring tribes. Senoi families typically begin the day with family dream interpretation and therapy, resolving conflicts of individual family members before they grow in intensity and aggressively expand into the larger fabric of their society. They believe that mastering the dream universe will bring peace and prosperity to their everyday lives (Stewart, 26–27).

The Shape of the Psyche: An Iceberg

Sigmund Freud rediscovered dreams for the modern world with his book *The Interpretation of Dreams* (1900), a comprehensive exploration of dreams and dream interpretation. Freud actually reaffirmed a very old concept, that dreams are meaningful and related to the health of the individual. He advanced dream theory by discovering the unconscious and describing its contents as material which we repress in our conscious life. His exploration of the unconscious realm was every bit as adventuresome and significant as ascending the highest peaks of the Himalayas.

It was discovered in the 1950s that at intervals during the night, a sleeping person has rapid eye movements (REM) and if awakened will report that he or she has been dreaming. Modern dream research is verifying what Freud earlier postulated: that dreaming is a universal human experience, occurring every night, whether we remember the dreams in the morning or not. And the process of dreaming seems to be linked to the growth and maturation of the individual personality.

The structure of the psyche can be compared to an iceberg: the conscious mind equals only that portion above the water; the rest of the iceberg floating in the cold, dark, mysterious depths—almost nine-tenths of the iceberg—represents the unconscious, a repository of past experiences. This huge mass is largely inaccessible to ordinary thinking, to just thinking-about-it. A mental censor stands at the boundary of the unconscious, preventing a flood of antisocial desires from flooding into one's consciousness and overpowering it. But during the night the censor relaxes, and some of the buried contents, disguised in symbol and metaphor, float upward, becoming the stuff of dreams.

Carl Jung recounts a dream about exploring a house. He began on the second story, which was decorated in an elaborate eighteenth-century style. As he descended, each story represented an earlier period in history. The ground floor had medieval furnishings; a stone stairway behind a heavy door led to the cellar:

> Examining the walls, I discovered layers of brick among the ordinary stone blocks, and ... knew that the walls dated from Roman times. My interest now was intense. I looked more closely at the floor. It was of stone slabs, and in one of these I discovered a ring. When I pulled it, the stone slab lifted, and again I saw a stairway of narrow stone steps leading down into the depths. These, too, I descended, and entered a low cave cut into the rock. Thick dust lay on the floor, and in the dust were scattered bones and broken pottery, like remains of a primitive culture. I discovered two

human skulls, obviously very old and half disintegrated. Then I awoke. (159)

Jung then explains that he believes that the house is an image of the psyche: the upper floor stands for the conscious portion, light and airy:

The ground floor stood for the first level of the unconscious. The deeper I went, the more alien and the darker the scene became. In the cave, I discovered remains of a primitive culture, that is, the world of the primitive man within myself—a world which can scarcely be reached or illuminated by consciousness. (160)

When these dreams are transformed into the traditional stories of a tribe or nation, we have mythology. Following Carl Jung, Joseph Campbell makes this connection: "Dream is the personalized myth, myth the depersonalized dream; both myth and dream are symbolic in the same general way of the dynamics of the psyche" (19–20). The symbiotic relationship between dream and myth clearly provides mechanisms for personal exploration: learning the language of myth is an entrée into dreams, and vice versa. Self-understanding and self-actualization can use both pathways, dreams and myths.

If you are called through the zenith
of the moon
and your soul is right for it
you emerge under a green sky
on blue earth.

There are large black cats
with white tipped claws
who speak of awesome events in Catland.

Now you are back
In a warm bed
surrounded by cool air
in the morning.

—Peter B./JH

When I was eleven, I sailed into the bowels of the earth and found incomparable beauty. In the heavy blackness the only sounds are the soft water noises beneath me and the loud hammering of my heart. Slowly, hesitantly, the heavens are born and I am surrounded by the flickering of a million soft blue stars, shimmering in strange swirling constellations. Beneath the water is a velvet darkness mutely reflecting the glory above. A small sound crashes into the silence and the universe vanishes, leaving me suspended in the moist darkness of the womb.

—Jenness G./C

Keeping a Dream Notebook

A basic principle of dreamwork is that the more you pay attention to your dreams, the more dream material you will remember. If at first you have trouble remembering your dreams, be patient and keep trying. Here are some hints:

1. Pay attention to the materials that float into consciousness during that twilight period just before sleep; this period can be very fruitful since the daytime censor is slowly loosening its grip.

2. Tell yourself before going to sleep that you will remember your dreams in the morning. This kind of autosuggestion is a way of paying attention, of alerting the memory, so to speak.

3. Jot down your dreams *immediately* upon awakening. Keep a notebook and pen beside your bed for this purpose. You may be able to find a pen with a small penlight attached for recording in the middle of the night. If you have to search the house for a pen that works, most dreams will ebb away. Let your consciousness drift into the first thing you remember in a dream and then write as quickly as possible. Another technique is to dictate your dream into a tape recorder. Once you have recorded the bare bones of a dream, it is possible to return to it later and fill in more details.

4. Freud recommended returning to dreams with the intention of filling in gaps, of elaborating or amplifying certain parts of the dream. He called this "secondary elaboration," and it should be done before interpretation takes place. Elaboration might involve relating your dream to other dreams or to myths, folktales, fairy tales, and legends.

Interpreting Your Dreams

1. Your dreams are your own creation; they are parts of you. It is more important to enjoy and value these creations of your inner life than to "correctly analyze" them. Your dreams may or may not have a discernible message, but generally dreams are in some way compensatory: that is, they are something that adds to or benefits your conscious awareness.

2. Interpreting dreams is a form of play (however serious); since dreams are expressed in image and symbol, they usually imply several things with several layers of meaning. There is *no single correct interpretation*. What is most important is what is meaningful or makes sense to the individual dreamer. Since dreams are

similar in some ways to myths, studying mythology aids in dream interpretation.

3. Usually it works best to record several dreams from several nights, and then begin interpretation by noting patterns of repetition, recurring characters, scenes, themes. Then ask the question "What are these patterns trying to tell me?" Recurring dreams are obviously important; they signal an ongoing concern of the unconscious.

4. Try reversing the images in the dream; turn them into their opposites and see if the dream makes more sense.

5. If a dream is unresolved, try finishing it the next night through suggesting its resolution just before sleep.

6. Fritz Perls, the originator of Gestalt Therapy, suggested a dream exercise: since everyone and everything in your dream is an aspect of you, carry on a dialogue with one of these parts as a means of understanding the dream's message. Again, you could suggest this dialogue to yourself as you nod off to sleep.

7. Enjoy your dreams. And share them. Dreams seem to increase in significance when they are shared with others. Gather together a few friends to meet in homes for an informal dream workshop. Begin each session by reading from your dream notebooks. At first this might feel intimidating, but the actual act of sharing brings a deep excitement, as if one were acknowledging a lost relative.

It seems only fitting that I conclude this section with one of my own dreams:

> I was walking through a busy street with jostling crowds and restaurants. Earlier I had kidded a fellow student about his bald head. We enter a restaurant and finally find a table and order. There is an older man with a bald head sitting across the room. I make a remark to him and he gets up pretending that he is angry, and makes his way through the tables towards me. When he gets close enough I reach up and hug him, and he hugs me. I say, "I really love you, you know." He says, "I know." He begins to return to his table, but turns and pulls at the top of my head, and a full wig lifts up a ways. He says, "Soppy, wet hair. And what's underneath it?" Everyone in the room is looking at me and laughing. He pulls the wig up, and under it, an identical head of hair. He says, "Soppy, wet hair, and under it? Soppy, wet hair." (5/79)

I am a dream, forgotten
At morning
As a nameless lover,
An unfulfilled prophesy,
A generic shopper,
A statistic

—Tanner P./C

I never remember dreams,
Only nightmares.
Actually,
Only 1 nightmare:
Coming home, and
finding that
my family moved and
left no forwarding address.

—Dee Dee H./HS

In 5th grade, one morning my mother told me all my blue jeans were dirty. She made me wear my sister's old girl's pants that were blue and glittery with a zipper on the side and no fly. Never have I been so humiliated, never have I suffered so much in front of friends. I was a prisoner in the skin of some female—I didn't know how to act.

DREAM . . . I am standing in an old empty house with just one chair which turns into a woman whom I seem to be acquainted with. I suddenly realize I am wearing woman's clothes. The woman with the black hair leads me through the empty house, up and down the stairs. All the time I am afraid someone will see me in my black dress, heels and other female attire. She is doing this on purpose to me.

—Albert R./C

Daydreams and Reveries

The happy childhood is filled with daydreams, when we sit on a grassy hill and float away into the parade of animals in the clouds. It is a form of escape, it is stretching the imagination, it is wondrously pleasurable.

The heavy streak of practicality in our society tends to make daydreaming the enemy of work. Work means productive activity, so just sitting around daydreaming isn't real work. Yet new ideas, inventions, visions come from someone just sitting around fishing with his or her imagination. Do poets do anything really useful? After all, they spend a great deal of time in a haze apparently doing nothing.

Daydreaming is the very essence of creativity: escaping from the old and mundane, from the prison of logic and common sense, in order to experience the new and the fantastic. Gaston Bachelard prefers the word *reverie*, the French roots of which mean "delirium" and "wandering":

> Certain poetic reveries are hypothetical lives which enlarge our lives by letting us in on the secrets of the universe. A world takes form in our reverie, and this world is ours. This dreamed world teaches us the possibilities for expanding our being within our universe. (Bachelard, 8)

Reverie requires a kind of letting go while still paying attention, and that is one description of the creative process. In an earlier chapter, I associated this process with stream of consciousness and automatic writing, and I said that using this process in writing requires practice. It is one thing to sit on top of a big rock and just let your mind wander, and another thing to face the blank page and string one image after another, one phrase after another.

This nectar-and-ambrosia of each fresh morning
fills the lazy blood, a music that slowly ripens
as the minutes ascend. You fear the space you live in,
it's brittle, will break like the crystal
of a watch. When you leave on your walk
to the campus, a redheaded bird follows, soaring
and weaving its baton of a body through the blue score,
footnotes that accompany pedestrians along their
daydreams.

—Gene Frumkin

My Own Dress Shop, Sweetie

See that cloud cushion rolling
over the hills, sweetie?
Those are the clouds I always
dreamed of. I dreamed of
a summer dwelling on the
coast at Monterrey, I dreamed of
a wing-backed, baby blue
T-Bird that would take me
away from here, like to holidays
in Cheyenne.
I dreamed of my very own dress
shop, sweetie.
One with big windows, and a
tree growing on the inside.

I had a red, white, and blue
awning that stretched all
across the storefront, and
a little poodle sleeping
beside the cash register.
I was all set, sweetie. I was
listening to the radio
and watching my customers
worry about skirt length.
I was watching those clouds
roll in, sweetie, from who knows where . . .
Maybe Cheyenne, maybe California,
like from a T-Bird
window. Pretty funny isn't it?
I mean it seems like I had
the best of all those dreams,
huh, sweetie . . .
all in one little dress shop.

—Jenny W./C

Monsters, Fairies, and UFOs

Open a door or window into the nighttime world and the world of daylight and sanity slowly begins to fill with mysterious shapes and eerie sounds. Monsters have always existed in the wilderness, beyond the reaches of law and order. Great sea creatures threatened early mariners; dragons guarded golden hoards in distant, rugged mountains; giants roamed the hills at the farthest edge of what was known.

And these monsters still patrol the fringes of our imagination. Hunters and hikers periodically catch a glimpse of Bigfoot or Sasquatch, the legendary apelike giant who roams the mountains of the West, from northern California to southern Alaska. The Abominable Snowman, large and hairy, is the Himalayan version of Bigfoot.

Some couples spend their vacation time camped with telescopes and cameras on the shores of Loch Ness, hoping to catch a glimpse of the watery monster inhabiting the dark depths of the lake. Not to be outdone, the Chinese in 1980 spotted a water monster living in a mountain lake, Tien Zhi ("Lake of Heaven"), in northeast China. Add to this collection all the nightmare creatures which have been spotted in dark alleys, all the shadowy shapes disappearing into the trees seen by campers in the forest. I call this phenomenon the "wilderness syndrome."

From earliest times, human beings have been prey to large animals. Monsters and giants were used to explain hallucinations and "unnatural" disasters, such as tidal waves, volcanic eruptions, and earthquakes. These natural and unnatural creatures were a testimony to the fragility of the cosmic order—how the balance of nature's forces could be upset at any time. Monsters were a stimulus to daily vigilance, and a reminder of human frailty.

Psychologists might be able to explain past sightings, but why is there such a serious interest in monsters today? An obvious answer is that these monsters actually exist and always have existed—at least enough of them to give credence to the whole body of stories about them. An alternative view is that our eyes and ears are not reliable guides to the line between the natural and the supernatural: we see and hear what we believe we can see and hear. Not "seeing is believing," but "believing is seeing."

Monsters also fulfill our wishes and fantasies. So much of life is humdrum and habitual, so much of the earth is tamed and domesticated, that it gives us pleasure to think that somewhere there is a region of freedom and barbarity, untainted by "thou shalt nots" and taxes. And then there is the notion that chaos does indeed lurk out there at the fringes of the last frontier, and that our civilization is fragile enough to crack asunder and be destroyed—an apocalyptic fear.

At the other extreme are all the stories about little people—fairies, elves, and brownies—who grant favors as well as play tricks. Ireland is famous for its leprechauns, who are often cobblers but are also the guardians of buried treasure. The nisse of Scandinavia are household spirits like the brownies of England and Scotland; they can be helpful but are also full of mischief. Trolls also come from Scandanavia and can be either gigantic or dwarfish; they are ogres who reside in darkness and guard hidden treasure. If monsters are splashed in large print across major disasters or fears, then little people are a testimony to the vagaries of daily existence.

Some would argue that both monsters and little people represent untapped dimensions of the psyche, and that their recurrence represents a warning to us that we need to explore the inner worlds of the unconscious before they erupt into some final cataclysm.

After these serious explanations, the best reason for monsters, giants, and fairies is that they are fun; they bring pleasure to the imagination while animating the landscape; they are a bridge between the seriousness of the daytime world and the fancies of the night.

I woke up
and there was a 50 foot corpse
with blue jeans and a T-shirt
that said "Eddie."

He had long hair and his skin
was like old leather with worms in it.
I picked up my frying pan—
all of a sudden his eyes glowed
and shot lightning.
It ricocheted off my pan and hit him
in the head, caught on fire,
burned to the ground.

The next morning I looked out
and the ground opened,
a tongue came out, pulled him in,
then it closed up.

—Jason H./JH

My father took me outside one day. I must have been five or six,
and we went out the back door to the woodpile. There, looking
tiny next to the pile, was a little house quickly nailed together for
a little shelter. It had a door and a window and a roof. He pointed
to it and told me that fairys lived there, and only at night. He said
that they would dance around and guard the woodpile.

From then on I would go and look at it alone. I remember getting on my hands and knees to look through the door. I could see
little piles of grass and nutshells, and I could look in the window.
I never told anyone about it.

—Gil S./C

The same range of comments that were made about monsters can
be made about UFOs and space creatures: they fulfill certain
psychological needs, and a few might even exist. In our confusion about
the destiny of this planet, it is comforting to imagine that somewhere
there is a race of beings who have solved the problems of human suffering and war.

For a number of years, New Mexico has been the focus of ufologists.
But why are extraterrestrials interested in this particular state? Theories
vary. One is that their spaceships refuel in highly magnetic places in
New Mexico. Others say that these cosmic foreigners are interested in
keeping track of weapons and energy research in Los Alamos and
Albuquerque, and the missile work at White Sands.

A common-sense explanation for the numerous sightings in New
Mexico and other large Western states is that the sparse population and
vast territory provide remote areas for clandestine landings and speculation. The big open sky at night is an ideal theater for citizens lonely
on the job, such as patroling sheriffs and solitary ranchers.

One of the most famous UFO cases occurred on April 24, 1964, just
outside Socorro, New Mexico. A police officer, Lonnie Zamora, was
chasing a speeder when he was distracted by an explosion; going to

investigate, he found a shiny spacecraft shaped like an egg and two small figures dressed in white coveralls. While he was radioing for aid, the craft whizzed off out of sight, leaving four impressions of the landing gear and burnt greasewood bushes. The event was reported in the world press, and thousands of the curious arrived in Socorro to investigate. Soon the landing site was trampled and all evidence was gone. Lonnie Zamora became the target of both UFO afficionados and skeptics.

---

        searching for creativity

i hear the ping
of deep submarines
deep within
my dirty dishwater

i hear the flutter
of moth's wings
against my shuttered windows
seeking a hidden light

i hear the flap
of lightning bats
playing loop-de-loop
behind my closet doors

trembling on cold tile
i peer into my bathwater
and see nebulous shapes
glide through my bright soapy sea

                        —Jon W./C

When I was five, my family moved from Los Angeles to Colorado. After four years in a city, I was returning to my birthplace.

Our original destination was Denver. We stopped in the village of San Luis for one night but ended that night by being convinced to stay in a nearby mountain cabin for a while. We stayed for four months.

After the years of city streets, city cars, city noises, and Disneyland, we used the water of the mountain. We were surrounded by the children of the mountain, prairie dog, blackbird, frog, and the bear. The bear seemed to guard over the wood and water I gathered.

When it was dark, before and during dreams I feared the bear. The owner of the cabin, Mr. Salasar, gave me a bear rug to sit on near the fire. It was a warm place during afternoon thunder showers and on foggy evenings. The bear of my dreams changed into one who also guarded me.

                        —Winston J./C

Long Distance Voyager

I climb into the capsule
the transporter with the hyperspace light
A little Straits on the radio.
ein bitte liten folkevognet.
The warmth of the motor
softly surrounds the creature
Churp, Churp little Beetle
away we go
into the sunset
"Remember to get milk."

—Thomas A./HS

The UFO

like a big lollipop without a stick
flying high in the sky.

—Kathy L./JH

Classroom Activities

Discussion Questions

1. In the fourth century B.C., the Chinese philosopher Chuang Tzu wondered about the relation of dream and reality. He said that he dreamed he was a butterfly flying around happily, enjoying life and not conscious of who he was. Suddenly he woke up and realized that he was Chuang Tzu, and then asked,

   Did I dream that I was a butterfly, or did
   the butterfly dream he was Chuang Tzu?

   What questions about the relationship between dream and reality are raised by Chuang Tzu's question?

2. Dreams can enlighten the present or point to the future. Have you had a dream which did either?

3. What constitutes a nightmare? Do most nightmares have common ingredients? Did you ever have a recurring nightmare?

4. Psychologists suggest that slips of the tongue, the phenomenon of deja vu, premonitions, and intuitive solutions to problems are evidence of the unconscious. Have you had a personal experience which would suggest the existence of the unconscious?

5. Suppose your boss, principal, supervisor, or parent would let you have the rest of the day off if you could convince him or her that you would do something exciting; what would you do?

6. Consider the command "Stop wasting time!" How is it possible to waste time? Did you know that someone has painted a detailed cathedral on a grain of rice? Was that a waste of time? Do you think there is any use for daydreaming in American society, or should the greater emphasis be placed on the practical and the material? Put together a campaign for more daydreaming and reverie (or, conversely, for a more hard-headed approach to life).

7. Some people take vacations in places that are different from the ordinary work routine at home. Living in the desert country of New Mexico, I love to visit the ocean and just sit and watch the water. What are your ideal vacation spots, whether you actually go there or not?

Writing Suggestions

1. With some practice you can treat your daydreams as if they were small dramas put on for you by your psyche. Are there stories which commonly appear in your daydreams? Can you identify the main characters? Write down one of these stories.

2. After recording your dreams for several nights, use the dream material as the basis of a poem. (It might be necessary to edit or elaborate on the original material.)

3. Write about an imaginary world. You might want to use music to set the mood. Write about the worst kind of place or the best.

4. Guided fantasies are situations that someone else (such as a teacher) sets up, and then the young writer completes the scene. The introduction might be a single sentence or a lengthy paragraph. Some possibilities:

   A. A man with dark glasses and a bulge under his coat walks into the airplane.
   B. What is the woman with the green hair doing at the motel?
   C. You are in a cave, and up ahead there is a scratching noise.
   D. A spaceship takes you captive.
   E. A sea monster just swallowed you and your boat.
   F. The mail carrier arrives and brings you a letter informing you that you have inherited a million dollars.
   G. A special machine can reduce you in size so that you can travel inside your own body.

Encourage the writer to be specific about sights and smells, the time of day, or the place. Details stimulate the imagination and help the fantasy to unfold.

5. What is your experience with ghosts and monsters? Are you aware of haunted houses or mysterious happenings? Write about them.
6. Draw a monster on the blackboard. Each student is to contribute a part of the monster. When the drawing is finished, write about it.

References

Bachelard, Gaston. 1971. *The Poetics of Reverie: Childhood, Language and the Cosmos.* Translated by Daniel Russell. Boston: Beacon Press.

Campbell, Joseph. 1956. *The Hero with a Thousand Faces.* New York: The World Publishing Company.

Freud, Sigmund. 1965 [1900]. *The Interpretation of Dreams.* Edited by J. Strachey. New York: Avon Books.

Jung, Carl G. 1963. *Memories, Dreams, Reflections.* Edited by Aniela Jaffé. New York: Vintage Books.

Merton, Thomas. 1970. *The Wisdom of the Desert: Sayings from the Desert Fathers of the Fourth Century.* New York: New Directions.

Sandars, N. K., trans. 1960. *The Epic of Gilgamesh.* Baltimore, Md.: Penguin Books.

Shakespeare, William. 1988. *The Tempest.* Edited by David Bevington. New York: Bantam Books.

Stewart, Kilton. 1972. "Dream Exploration among the Senoi." In *Sources: An Anthology of Contemporary Materials Useful for Preserving Personal Sanity While Braving the Great Technological Wilderness,* edited by Theodore Roszak, 20–39. New York: Harper & Row.

12 A Matter of Death and Life

Images attached to death are imprinted in our consciousness, shaping our attitudes and actions: the skull and crossbones, Father Time with his scythe, an hourglass, "dust to dust," heaven and hell, ghosts and skeletons, cancer and mushroom clouds. There are also the images of spinning, measuring, and cutting the thread of life, associated with the Fates in ancient Greek religion.

Death raises so many issues that it is helpful to divide the topic into two broad categories: (1) death as a national and global issue, involving pollutants, genocide, and nuclear holocaust. In a very real sense, we live in the age of death. And (2) death as an individual issue. Awareness of our mortality leads to questions about the meaning of life, the effects of our death on the living, the possibility of an afterlife, and the consolation of religion. The fact that uncertainty and the unknown are intertwined with our mortality makes death a great mystery.

In the face of death, poetry has several roles to play. While it can be a reminder of the presence of death, poetry can also enrich our lives with solace, celebration, and visions of the future.

The Age of Death

Death is the X in the universe, the inevitable clinker, the great equalizer. For many thousands of years it has raised the ultimate questions for religion and philosophy. Unlike all the other animals, humans can probe the mysteries of death, and resist—even deny—its ultimate claim. With Job, we wonder about a world in which the young and the innocent suffer and die.

World War I, World War II and the Holocaust, Stalin's massacres, the purges in China, the killing fields in Cambodia, prison camps, and revolutions around the globe—just a partial list suggests the power of death in the twentieth century, more powerful than any time since the Middle Ages.

Despite medical advances and high technology, despite our concerns with security and order, we are surrounded by images and accounts

162

of death and destruction; TV and newspapers are preoccupied with killings and violence at home and abroad, with terrorism and insurrection, and with speculation about nuclear war and the death of our planet, either by sudden catastrophe or gradual contamination. All school-age children have been brought up in the climate of the Cold War, which floats like a poisonous cloud at the edge of our consciousness.

As we approach the end of this century there is increasing talk about a major catastrophe, the Armageddon or some other apocalypse. Are we projecting the fears and monsters of our inner, spiritual life onto the world landscape?

Mortality and Metaphor

The ancient Greeks resorted to metaphor to describe the awesome power of death to wipe out an entire army or to unexpectedly and disastrously intervene in a secure family situation. The Fates, in the guise of three sisters, could strike at any time: Clotho spins the thread of life for each individual; Lachesis measures the length of the threads; and Atropos cuts them off with her metaphysical shears.

We resort to concepts such as fate to indicate the unpredictable aspect of death, but the physical act of dying can also be complicated. In the past a feather was held under the nose or a mirror in front of the mouth to determine respiration. Death occurred when the heart stopped or when breathing stopped. In later years, the absence of brain waves became another sign of death. But with modern technology it is possible to keep patients "alive" on machines by forcing the heart to beat and the lungs to inhale and expel air while the top part of the brain, which controls consciousness, memory, sight and smell, is dead. This possibility has raised both ethical and legal questions for our society, and has caused anguish and financial stress for the relatives of a patient connected to a machine. Who pulls the plug on such a machine? When is the plug pulled?

Is death an absence of life or an external force that comes after us and overtakes us? John Steinbeck describes our intuition of death:

> Do we smell the disintegrating cells? Do we see the hair losing its luster and uneasy against the scalp, and the skin dropping its tone? We do not know these reactions one by one, but we say, that man or cat or dog or cow is going to die. If the fleas on a dog know it and leave their host in advance, why do not we also know it? Approaching death, the pre-death of the cells, has informed the fleas and us too. (186)

The gypsy Pilar in Hemingway's *For Whom the Bell Tolls* is more specific about the odor of death which hung about a bullfighter on the day he was to be killed in the ring. She tells Robert Jordan how to recognize the smell of death as a combination of several smells: the brass handle of a locked porthole on a rolling ship; the kiss of an old woman who has just sipped the blood of beasts at the slaughterhouse; a pailful of dead chrysanthemums; and, finally, the smells of the houses of prostitution on a misty day mixed with a gunnysack smelling of wet earth, rotting flowers, and lovemaking—as if the smell of death were a mixture of "little deaths."

In "The Death of Ivan Ilyich," Tolstoy uses the metaphor of blackness to visually represent Ivan Ilyich's slow death from a cancerous tumor:

> He struggled in that black sack into which he was being thrust by an invisible, resistless force. He struggled as a man condemned to death struggles in the hands of the executioner, knowing that he cannot save himself. And every moment he felt that despite all his efforts he was drawing nearer and nearer to what terrified him. He felt that his agony was due to his being thrust into that black hole and still more to his not being able to get right into it.... Suddenly some force struck him in the chest and side, making it still harder to breathe, and he fell through the hole and there at the bottom was a light. (154)

Phrases used for death either bring its reality closer or actually distance us from it: "passed away," "quit the scene," "passed on," "went to a better life," "just sleeping," "passed through the curtain," "bought the farm," "went to her reward," "bit the dust." These euphemisms indicate perceptions of and attitudes toward death: is it frightening, mysterious, the final act, or simply a transition?

The fear of death inevitably spawns grim humor about the Grim Reaper, as if death itself were a kind of joke played on humans by the gods. It is said that when the famous writer Gertrude Stein was dying, Alice B. Toklas drew near the deathbed and, desiring news about the afterlife, urgently asked, "Gertrude . . . what is the answer?" "Alice," responded Gertrude, "Alice, . . . what was the question?" And then she died.

Fear also spawns denial. In the United States, we have tried to shut out the aging process and death with our cultish devotion to youth and health, to cosmetics and surgery, as if we were grasping for immortality on earth. Where else but in California would you find the Center for Cryonics? Cryonics is the deep-freezing of bodies immediately after death, with the hope that technology a hundred years hence will be able to revive and repair the deceased.

Dying

Holding your breath under water
for long periods of time.
Sleeping
for time eternal
a candle
suddenly snuffed out.
Then darkness
silence enveloping you.
You want to scream
but you are stifled.
You try to reach out
grasp someone's hand
have a feeling of warm
flesh & blood,
but your hand doesn't move.

—Eric J./JH

A Sickening Question

Pain, Numbness, Confusion
How could he be sick?
How could he lose his leg?
How could he die?
And what I want to know is this—
How do you take revenge on a cancer cell?

—Steve W./HS

?
Death
Is
A
Question Mark
?

—Chris K./JH

Although my mother died when I was twelve, my first real contact with death was in a hospital surgery ward where I worked as a nurse's aide. We began an emergency heart case about one a.m., just as I was finishing my shift. I helped the man onto the operating table from his stretcher and left a short time later for home. When I returned for work the next afternoon at four o'clock, the same case was still going. Uncountable pints of blood and tubes had been used up. They had to locate a third case of plasma from outside the hospital. They worked until late evening, but finally gave up after nineteen hours.

I was sent for a shroud and identification tags. His body was so bloated and large from the intake of fluids that the shroud did not quite fit, and he weighed much more than he had before. It took four of us to lift him into the morgue pan, and when we slid the pan and body into the locker and shut it, I could only see him as he had been the day before. Alive, thinking, talking, breathing; it was hard to imagine how it would be to be shut in a drawer and later burned or buried.

—Ford D./C

The Death Journey

Living about 60,000 years ago, the Neanderthals buried their dead. Archeologists have uncovered Neanderthal graves that contained weapons, tools, and food offerings; the bodies were placed in a sleeping or fetal position with an east-west orientation. They claim that this evidence shows that the Neanderthals believed in an afterlife and that the journey to the other world required food and weapons. The body positions suggested that death was seen as being analogous to sleep (see Howell, *Early Man*).

Early humans might also have used the analogy of the sun, which is born in the east, passes overhead from east to west, and dies, only to be reborn the following morning. Or perhaps they used the phases of the moon as an analogy of death and rebirth. For whatever reason, many cultures conceive of life as a journey, a pilgrimage, a pathway, which does not end with death, but continues in a different realm or dimension. For the Greeks, death was a journey into Hades, an underworld which was elaborated into regions of reward and punishment by the time of the Romans.

The Roman writer Cicero (106–43 B.C.) looked forward to warm reunions after death in the essay "On Old Age":

> From this life I depart as from a temporary lodging, not as from a home. For nature has assigned it to us as an inn to sojourn in, not a place of habitation. Oh, glorious day! when I shall depart to that divine company and assemblage of spirits, and quit this troubled and polluted scene. For I shall go not only to those great men of whom I have spoken before, but also to my friend Cato, than whom never was better man born, nor more distinguished for pious affection. (62–63)

Cerements and Rituals

If the nature of death is tinged with uncertainty and variety, so is our handling of it in ceremony and attitude.

Members of certain monastic orders are said to sleep every night in their coffins. The Greek root of the word *coffin* is *kophinos*, meaning "basket," but in Christian symbolism climbing into the coffin is a *regressus ad uterum*: the coffin symbolizes the mystic womb of rebirth—resurrection. Some people regularly visit their cemetery plots, as well as those of the deceased. Occasionally families end up in court quarreling about who will rest throughout all eternity next to the parents.

The word *cemetery* comes from the Greek *koimeterion*, meaning "sleeping place." The word *cerement*, referring to the shroud used for wrapping a dead body, comes from *cerecloth*, whose root, *cere*, comes from the Greek *keros*, wax, and therefore points back to a time when cloth treated with wax was used for wrapping the body—no doubt as a preservative. One is reminded of the Egyptian process of mummification, as well as the contemporary practice of placing bodies in expensive airtight and watertight vaults. In many places on earth, land is so scarce that cemeteries must be constructed above ground, with the containers for the dead stacked three and four high. Other cultures, for religious and other reasons, cremate the dead instead of burying them.

Death causes a rupture in the social fabric, and religious ritual is directed toward the repair and perpetuation of community, faith, and hope. Funerals are therefore as much for the living as for the dead. Irish wakes are famous for the element of bonding together the living while mourning the deceased.

In 1984–85 a major exhibit on death was held in the Children's Museum in Boston. Children could listen to dirges, touch a plastic-coated dead frog, look into a coffin, compare bloated, bullet-ridden bodies from El Salvador with the make-believe violence on a TV Western, watch a speeded-up film of a dead mouse being devoured by maggots, and see the burial robes from various religions. Exhibits had signs such as "Dying isn't a vacation. It's not like going to visit your grandmother. You don't come back again." "Everything that is alive now will die, decompose, and return to life," and slang or euphemistic terms such as "Put to sleep," "Six feet under," "Belly up," and "Croaked."

No matter how you feel about this museum project, the idea of it is quite incredible. Has death become so far removed from ordinary urban life, so hidden in the recesses of hospitals and nursing homes, that a museum feels compelled to reveal its varied faces in an exhibit?

From ancient China (4th century B.C.) comes this story:

> When Chuang Tzu's wife died, Hui Tzu went to the home to participate in the rites of mourning. He was surprised to find Chuang Tzu drumming on an upside down bowl on his knees and singing a song.
>
> "After all," said Hui Tzu, "she lived with you, raised your children, and grew old with you. It is shocking enough that you do not mourn for her, but you go too far when your friends find you drumming and singing!"
>
> "You misunderstand and misjudge me," said Chuang Tzu. "When my wife died, I felt awful, as any man would. But soon I began

to think about what had happened, and it came to me that death is not something unnatural and strange.

"In the beginning, before life there was form, and before form there was spirit. We were blended in the one great homogenous mass. Then a time came when the mass evolved spirit, spirit evolved form, form evolved life. And now life in its turn has evolved death. Like nature humans have their seasons, the passage from spring to summer, from autumn to winter.

"If someone is tired and has gone to lie down, we do not follow after him with shouting and crying. The person I have lost has gone to sleep for a while in the Great Inner Room. To disturb her rest with the sounds of grief would show that I knew nothing about nature's Sovereign Law. That is why I no longer mourn." (retold from Waley, 6–7)

Some may think of death
as a day of joy
for the dead person
gets to touch the face of God.
                    —David G./JH

              For Nancy Palmyra Boyd
                    (1872–1961)

Sometimes
when trains rumble
along margins of the night
I wake up
wanting to write you a letter
little grandmother

you who rode with me
on long trains through my childhood

who told me life
would be ringed with dark edges

wanting to tell you

how white the dogwood bloomed
that spring you did not live to see

how the new moon is still
a knife-slice of raw pearl
even here in New Mexico
this place you could not imagine

I want to tell you
there were trains
I should have taken

there have been
dark edges
                              —Jeanne Shannon

El Dia Del Muerto

1. Three blocks east of the plaza is Rosas
   no funeral too large no service too small
   open day and night week in week out.
   Ashes on the tile floor, pea green walls
   an aged stuffed chair for waiting.

2. Tito's mother accidentally killed
   two of her children, she was up tight
   her lover was late
   Refugio's oldest fell down a well
   uncovered in the backyard when he was six
   and Jorge not yet two swallowed rat poison
   was fatally bitten, caught a deadly virus
   it's not clear.

3. We sat some time together
   watching the local borrachos
   dancing with brooms and wives
   spilling their beer.
   I asked about his work, his family
   he held a colored slide to the light
   an only daughter after seven sons
   lay quietly on velvet plush.
   His eyes were like two weathered oaks
   in a storm, he shook my hand
   pushing his hat forward towards the night.

4. Shelves cover the walls in Rosas
   caskets floor to ceiling
   most are white, short, three to four feet long
   both plain and fancy, scrolled in gold
   with and without handles.

—David Johnson

Life-in-Death/Death-in-Life

No matter how hard we try to separate life and death, no matter how
much we try to isolate death as some implacable enemy or some reluc-
tant friend, life and death are intertwined like the strands of a piece
of rope. Life feeds on other life; one life is sustained by another's death.
The same gullet that feeds is the death canal for the food. The Japanese
have a myth that illustrates this connection:

> The Moon god was sent down to Earth . . . to see that the Food
> deity, Uke-Mochi, was performing her duties. In order to enter-
> tain this higher being . . . Uke-Mochi opened her mouth while facing
> the fields and boiled rice streamed from it. When she faced the
> sea, fish and edible seaweed were regurgitated, and when she faced
> the wooded hills, game of various kinds came forth. The Moon god
> was, understandably, unappreciative of the manner in which the

repast was served, and so violent was his anger that he killed the unfortunate Uke-Mochi. However, even in death her body continued its work, for cows and horses emerged from her head, silkworms from her eyebrows, millet grew from her forehead and a rice plant sprang from her stomach. (Piggott, 19)

This kind of story, about providing food through the death of a god or goddess, is common throughout the world. It illustrates the necessity of sacrifice for the next generation, and the inescapable link between death and life. Whatever else might happen to our minds or spirits, our bodies are inescapably mortal, and mortality means *food* for sustenance and *sexuality* for reproduction and eventually *death* for each individual. In story after story, food, sex, and death form the archetypal triangle, the essential fabric of mortality. As we toss these ideas around, we become increasingly aware of paradox and the limits of understanding. Beyond reason are those moments when some intimation warms the consciousness, when past enemies become friends. Octavio Paz re-creates such a reconciling moment:

By the sea or before a mountain, lost among the trees of a forest or at the entrance to a valley that spreads out at our feet, our first sensation is strangeness or separation. We feel different. The natural world presents itself as something alien, possessing an existence of its own. This estrangement soon turns into hostility. Each branch of the tree speaks a language we do not understand; from each thicket a pair of eyes spies on us; unknown creatures threaten or mock us. And the opposite may occur: nature turns inward and the sea heaves and plunges before us, indifferently; the rocks become even more dense and impenetrable; the desert, more vacuous and inaccessible. We are nothing in relation to so much existence turned in on itself. And from this feeling that we are nothing we proceed, if contemplation is prolonged and panic does not overtake us, to the opposite state: the rhythm of the sea keeps time with that of our blood; the silence of the rocks is our own silence; to walk among the sands is to walk through the span of our consciousness, as boundless as they; the forest murmurs allude to us. We are all part of all. Being emerges from nothing. The same rhythm moves us, the same silence surrounds us. The very objects are animated, and as the Japanese poet Buson so happily puts it:

Before the white chrysanthemums
the scissors hesitate
for an instant.

That instant reveals the unity of being. All is still and all is in motion. Death is not a thing apart: it is, in an inexpressible way, life. The revelation of our nothingness leads us to the creation of being. (137)

Poems do not conceal the human condition but reveal it. Unlike religion, which must provide answers for the reality of death, and unlike philosophy, which must digest the rational limits of religion's answers, poetry creates the image of life and death together. Death is not the denial of poetry but an accessory to the poem's celebration of life: yes, the autumn brings the harvest of wheat and heroes alike. And yes, the spring erupts with tender shoots and children dance with immortality in their limbs.

A primary goal of art and poetry is to discover, within the dark earth of death, the bursting seed of new life. I think of Dixieland bands in New Orleans accompanying the casket with dirges on the way to the cemetery, but breaking into celebration and joy on the route home. Mexicans celebrate the Day of the Dead with a torchlight parade into the cemetery at night and a picnic on the gravestones.

With the transforming power of the imagination, grief and loss are turned into sustaining images for the living. Continually and always, the challenge of creation is to bring new life out of old, to reweave the fabric of communal life out of all that is broken and disconnected.

[The following eulogy was written in 1976 by Scott Lee Sanchez, nine years old. He wrote the poem for his father, a fire fighter who died in a supermarket blaze. It was read by the fire chaplain at the funeral.]

Life

Life is the sun that gives us light.
Life is the stars that shine at night.
Life is the soil that makes the plants grow.
But the answer to life, no one knows.

Life is the sun that lights the sky.
Life is the moon that's floating by.
Life, dear life, that's on what we rely.
Life is the answer to when and why

Life is the sun that gives us light.
Life is the stars that shine at night.
Life is each and every breath.
Life is not only life, it is also death.

Back into My Body

My mother is dying.

I giver her a bath/she's pregnant
with death
swollen belly and one nipple
gone
where I bit down as a baby.

I'm taking her back into my body.

My mother is pulling
silk
from the cocoon
not to lose the thread.
She's larva again.

She's taken her hands
from my shoulders
no longer yells,
"Straighten up!"
Death has come to take her back
and only the well
pass blame.

Worms are at work in her veins.

Only the beautiful
hide their breasts and you
naked as a spool
have arranged the linens
for one last time
and touched the cranberry glass.

In the fight for your antiques
leave me nothing.
I'm alive
and strong with you back in my spine.
I lift you from your bath

and dry
and love you.

                              —Glenna Luschei

                    Death

You are not an invited guest
You are the unwelcome relative
that lives in the spare room

You hover near the kitchen stove
You watch me in my bath
You follow me to the hospital
to be near the surgeon's scalpel
You ride with me in the car

Don't steal glances at my grandchildren
they are too young
Be patient now
and watch me grow old
It won't be long 'til you show me the way
no need to worry
you'll always be employed.

                              —Ingerid Clugston

[The last poem is by the famous anthropologist and author of *Ishi in Two Worlds*, Theodora Kroeber-Quinn, who died of cancer in 1979 at the age of 82.]

Poem for the Living

When I am dead
Cry for me a little.
Think of me sometimes
But not too much.
It is not good for you
Or your wife or your husband
Or your children
To allow your thoughts to dwell
Too long on the Dead.
Think of me now and again
As I was in life
At some moment
It is pleasant to recall.
But not for long.
Leave me in peace
As I shall leave
You, too, in peace.
While you live
Let your thoughts be with
The Living.

Classroom Activities

Discussion Questions

1. Think about phrases used to indicate death, such as "passed away." Why do we use these euphemisms?

2. There are innumerable poems carved on gravestones in cemeteries. Classes might visit a cemetery in search of poems and symbols, and learn about the nature and purpose of cemeteries. It was once believed that the spirits of the deceased resided in their grave sites. I usually bring a gravestone rubbing to class to open discussion about symbols such as the hourglass, the scythe, sun and moon, ouroboros (a snake with its tail in its mouth), naked bones, skeleton, angels, door.

3. Why do we celebrate Memorial Day in the United States?

4. Two of the strongest poems in the English language about death were written by the Welsh poet Dylan Thomas: "Do Not Go Gentle into that Good Night," "And Death Shall Have No Dominion." Listen to Thomas read these poems on tape or record. See also John Donne's "No man is an island," *Meditation* XVII.

5. Earlier in this chapter the various parts of the odor of death, according to the gypsy Pilar in Hemingway's *For Whom the Bell Tolls*, are listed. Does death have some kind of presence that can be sensed?

6. In Gladstone, Michigan, there is the largest pet casket company in the world. The Pharaohs of ancient Egypt had a cemetery for cats, and the early Chinese emperors had dog cemeteries in Peking. There are pet cemeteries in California, Florida, Pennsylvania, and Ohio. Our backyard is our pet cemetery. How should the death of pets be treated?

7. Mortuaries used to provide datebooks for prospective customers. I thought that this was quite subtle and wrote the following:

> Keeping in Touch
> Mortuaries furnish their friends
> with black books
> your name in gold letters.
> Not a single ad inside—
> just the year divided into each day
> a tiny sunset on every page.

How should mortuaries advertise their services?

8. Two important books are Elisabeth Kübler-Ross's *On Death and Dying* and Jane Jacobs's *The American Way of Death*. A number of books have also been published on near-death experiences, such as Raymond Moody's *Life after Life*. Are our cultural attitudes about death changing?

Writing Suggestions

1. Here are two epitaphs from gravestones, minus the names:

> Entered life Via Baltimore
> Exited Via Albuquerque
> Beautiful spirit free from all stain
> Ours the heartache, sorrow and pain
> Thyne is the glory and infinite gain
> Thy slumber is sweet.

Write an epitaph for yourself.

2. If death is like a face or an object, draw it on the blackboard; each student could add a single feature. Write a poem from the picture.

3. What images do you associate with death? The use of a simile can help: "Death is like . . . ," as in "Death is like winter." This stem

can be repeated in each line. Other phrases include "I met death . . .," "I saw death . . .," "Death came . . . ."

Death is like . . .

a cold, dark room
an old rocking chair
as dark as an old closet
the final frontier
a pit, an endless pit
passing through a curtain
a matter of time
like a burned out bulb
dust under your bed

—JH students

4. Poetry is a good medium for writing eulogies. Write a eulogy for someone in your family, living or dead. Write a eulogy for yourself.

5. Imagine that because of disease or impending disaster to the planet, you have a limited amount of time yet to live, such as three days or one month. Imagine also that you have unlimited resources for your plans: what will you do?

6. "Occasional poems" are poems written for a specific occasion. I was visiting a class when the regular teacher's brother was killed in a car accident; I helped the class write a group poem for the occasion. When the space shuttle Challenger exploded (January 1986), I assigned this event to my poetry workshop. Is there some recent event worthy of a poem?

References

Cicero, Marcus Tullius. 1896. *Cicero's Old Age and Friendship*. Translated by Cyrus R. Edmonds. Philadelphia: David McKay, Publisher.

Howell, F. Clark, and the Editors of Time-Life Books. 1973. *Early Man*. New York: Time-Life Books.

Paz, Octavio. 1973. *The Bow and the Lyre*. Translated by Ruth L. C. Simms. New York: McGraw-Hill.

Piggott, Juliet. 1969. *Japanese Mythology*. London: Paul Hamlyn.

Steinbeck, John. 1952. *The Log from the Sea of Cortez*. New York: Random House.

Tolstoy, Leo. 1960. *"The Death of Ivan Ilyich" and Other Stories*. Translated by Almer Maude. New York: New American Library.

Waley, Arthur. 1939. *Three Ways of Thought in Ancient China*. Garden City, N.Y.: Doubleday & Company.

Author

 **David M. Johnson** is vitally interested in the role of storytelling in people's lives and in the role of mythology in culture. An associate professor of English at the University of New Mexico, he is a cofounder and former director of the Creative Writing Program there. Professor Johnson has conducted numerous workshops in elementary and secondary schools throughout New Mexico and the region, encouraging students to pursue the materials of their own experience in order to create stories that connect them to their personal and collective histories. He was coeditor of the *San Marcos Review* and is a current editor of the *Blue Mesa Review*. In addition to poems and articles published in regional and national journals, he has published three books of poetry: *Pilgrim Country, The Oldest Song,* and *Altar to an Unknown God.*